Elasticsearch Indexing

Improve search experiences with Elasticsearch's powerful indexing functionality – learn how with this practical Elasticsearch tutorial packed with tips!

Hüseyin Akdoğan

[PACKT] open source*
PUBLISHING   community experience distilled

BIRMINGHAM - MUMBAI

Elasticsearch Indexing

First published: December 2015

Production reference: 1171215

Published by Packt Publishing Ltd.

Livery Place

35 Livery Street

Birmingham B3 2PB, UK.

ISBN 978-1-78398-702-3

www.packtpub.com

Credits

Author
Hüseyin Akdoğan

Reviewer
John M. Petrone

Commissioning Editor
Kartikey Pandey

Acquisition Editor
Shaon Basu

Content Development Editor
Anish Dhurat

Technical Editor
Pranjali Mistry

Copy Editor
Neha Vyas

Project Coordinator
Bijal Patel

Proofreader
Safis Editing

Indexer
Mariammal Chettiyar

Graphics
Disha Haria

Production Coordinator
Nilesh Mohite

Cover Work
Nilesh Mohite

About the Author

Hüseyin Akdoğan began his software adventure with the GwBasic programming language. He started learning the Visual Basic language after QuickBasic and developed many applications until 2000, after which he stepped into the world of Web with PHP. After this, he came across Java! In addition to counseling and training activities since 2005, he developed enterprise applications with JavaEE technologies. His areas of expertise are JavaServer Faces, Spring Frameworks, and big data technologies such as NoSQL and Elasticsearch. Along with these, he is also trying to specialize in other big data technologies. Hüseyin also writes articles on Java and big data technologies and works as a technical reviewer of big data books. He was a reviewer of one of the bestselling books, *Mastering Elasticsearch – Second Edition*.

About the Reviewer

John M. Petrone is a veteran technology leader and innovator who has over 20 years of experience in leading software development and technical operations at organizations ranging in size and scope from early-stage start-ups to public companies and large system integrators. He's passionate about the strategic application of leading-edge technologies to solve real-world problems.

John is currently the CTO of LaunchPad Central, a SaaS platform company offering end-to-end solutions that help organizations innovate more efficiently and accelerate time to market new products. He runs the the engineering and product groups, where he heads the ongoing design, development, and operation of their SaaS products that enable high throughput innovation at scale.

Previously, John was the first CTO of Zignal Labs, a leader in delivering data-driven insights from real-time media monitoring and big data analytics. He recruited the original engineering team and designed, architected, and led the building of a real-time analytics platform. This platform ingests tens of millions of news stories, blog entries, and social media posts every day.

Prior to Zignal, John served as the SVP and CTO of Autobytel Inc (ABTL) from 2003-2008 and again from 2010-2012. He is the awarding-winning pioneer of online car buying and automotive marketing services, and he has led all technology activities and initiatives, including new product development, technical operations, and integration of acquired technologies. He was selected as one of the Premier 100 IT Leaders of 2006 by Computerworld Magazine.

John was also EVP and CTO of Preview Travel, Inc. from 1995 to 1999, where he built the team and platform and led them through a successful IPO in November 1997. Prior to Preview, he held senior technology positions at Oracle, Lotus Consulting, Price Waterhouse, and Andersen Consulting. John attended the University of Maryland, where he received a BS degree in aerospace engineering. He is also a graduate of the Executive Education Program at the UCLA Anderson School of Management.

www.PacktPub.com

Support files, eBooks, discount offers, and more

For support files and downloads related to your book, please visit www.PacktPub.com.

Did you know that Packt offers eBook versions of every book published, with PDF and ePub files available? You can upgrade to the eBook version at www.PacktPub.com and as a print book customer, you are entitled to a discount on the eBook copy. Get in touch with us at service@packtpub.com for more details.

At www.PacktPub.com, you can also read a collection of free technical articles, sign up for a range of free newsletters and receive exclusive discounts and offers on Packt books and eBooks.

https://www2.packtpub.com/books/subscription/packtlib

Do you need instant solutions to your IT questions? PacktLib is Packt's online digital book library. Here, you can search, access, and read Packt's entire library of books.

Why subscribe?

- Fully searchable across every book published by Packt
- Copy and paste, print, and bookmark content
- On demand and accessible via a web browser

Free access for Packt account holders

If you have an account with Packt at www.PacktPub.com, you can use this to access PacktLib today and view 9 entirely free books. Simply use your login credentials for immediate access.

Table of Contents

Preface   **v**

Chapter 1: Introduction to Efficient Indexing   **1**

Getting started   **2**
Understanding the document storage strategy   **2**
  The _source field   3
  The difference between the storable and searchable field   6
Analysis   **10**
Summary   **15**

Chapter 2: What is an Elasticsearch Index   **17**

Nature of the Elasticsearch index   **17**
  Indices   17
  Mapping   19
  Types   19
Document   **20**
  Denormalization   21
  Inverted index   23
Summary   **25**

Chapter 3: Basic Concepts of Mapping   **27**

Basic concepts and definitions   **27**
  Metadata fields   28
    _source   28
    _all   28
    _timestamp   30
    _ttl   32
Types   **33**
  Object type   33
    Root object type   37
  Attachment type   38

The relationship between mapping and relevant search results	38
Understanding the schema-less	43
Summary	45
Chapter 4: Analysis and Analyzers	**47**
Introducing analysis	47
Process of analysis	49
Built-in analyzers	50
Building blocks of Analyzer	51
Character filters	51
HTML Strip Char filter	51
Pattern Replace Char filter	53
Tokenizer	53
Token filters	54
What's text normalization?	55
ICU analysis plugin	56
ASCII Folding Token filter	56
An Analyzer Pipeline	60
Specifying the analyzer for a field in the mapping	60
Creating a custom analyzer	64
Summary	65
Chapter 5: Anatomy of an Elasticsearch Cluster	**67**
Basic concepts	67
Node	68
Non-data nodes	68
Dedicated master nodes	68
Client nodes	68
Tribe node	69
Shards	69
Replicas	69
Explaining the architecture of distribution	70
Correctly configuring the cluster	73
Choosing the right amount of shards and replicas	76
Summary	77
Chapter 6: Improving Indexing Performance	**79**
Configuration	80
Memory configuration	80
The ES_HEAP_SIZE environment variable	81
Avoiding swapping	82
Mlockall property	83
Garbage collector	84
The structure of JVM memory	84

What is the problem?	86
Monitoring garbage collection	86
VisualVM	87
Different strategies among garbage collectors	89
Process of deallocating memory	89
Types of garbage collector	89
File descriptors	**91**
Increasing FD limit on Unix systems	91
Optimization of mapping definition	**94**
Norms	**94**
Feature index_option of string type	**95**
Exclude unnecessary fields	**96**
Extension of the automatic index refresh time	**97**
Segments and merging policies	**98**
Choosing the right merge policy	**100**
Tiered policy	100
log_byte_size policy	102
Log_doc policy	103
The optimize API	**103**
Store module	**104**
Store types	**104**
Simple filesystem store	104
New IO filesystem store	105
MMap filesystem store	105
Hybrid filesystem store	106
Throttling I/O operations	**106**
Throttling type	106
Bulk API	**107**
Bulk sizing	**108**
Notes	**108**
Summary	**109**
Chapter 7: Snapshot and Restore	**111**
Snapshot repository	**111**
Repository types	**112**
Shared filesystem repository	112
URL repository	113
Cloud repository	114
HDFS filesystem repository	114
Snapshot	**114**
Restore	**118**
Overriding index settings during restore	**119**
How does the snapshot process works?	**120**
Summary	**122**

Chapter 8: Improving the User Search Experience   123

Correction of users' spelling mistakes   124
Suggesters   125
Using the _suggest REST endpoint   125
Suggest object inclusion in the query   127
Term suggester   128
Configuring the term suggester   129
The phrase suggester   131
Configuring the phrase suggester   133
The completion suggester   136
Mapping the configuration for the completion suggester   137
Indexing on completion field   138
Get suggestions   139
Improving the relevancy of search results   140
Boosting the query   140
Bool query   144
Synonyms   147
Be careful about the _all field   149
Summary   150
Index   151

Preface

The world that we live in is hungry for speed, efficiency, and accuracy. We want quick results and faster without compromising the accuracy. This is exactly why I have written this book. I have penned down my years of experience in this book to give you an insight into how to use Elasticsearch more efficiently in today's big data world. This book is targeted at experienced developers who have used Elasticsearch before and want to extend their knowledge about how to effectively perform Elasticsearch indexing. While reading this book, you'll explore different topics, all of which connect to efficient indexing and relevant search results in Elasticsearch. We will focus on understanding the document storage strategy and analysis process in Elasticsearch. This book will help you understand what is going on behind the scenes when you send a document for indexing or make a query. In addition, this book will ensure correct understanding of the meaning of schemaless by asking the question—is the claim that Elasticsearch stands for the schema-free model always true? After this, you will learn the analysis process and about analyzers. More importantly, this book will elaborate the relationship between data analysis and relevant search results. By the end of this book, I believe you will be in a position to master and unleash this beast of a technology.

What this book covers

Chapter 1, *Introduction to Efficient Indexing*, will introduce you to the document storage strategy and the basic concepts related to the analysis process.

Chapter 2, *What is an Elasticsearch Index*, describes the concept of Elasticsearch Index, how the inverted index mechanism works, why you should use data denormalization, and what its benefits. In addition to this, it explains dynamic mapping and index flexibility.

Chapter 3, *Basic Concepts of Mapping*, describes the basic concepts and definitions of mapping. It answers the question what is the relationship between mapping and relevant search results questions. It explains the meaning of schemaless. It also covers metadata fields and data types.

Chapter 4, Analysis and Analyzers, describes analyzers and the analysis process of Elasticsearch, what tokenizers, the character and token filters, how to configure a custom analyzer and what text normalization is. This chapter also describes the relationship between data analysis and relevant search results.

Chapter 5, Anatomy of an Elasticsearch Cluster, covers techniques to choose the right number of shards and replicas and describes a node, the shard concept, replicas, and how shard allocation works. It also explains the architecture of data distribution.

Chapter 6, Improving Indexing Performance, covers how to configure memory, how JVM garbage collector works, why garbage collector is so important for performance, and how to start tuning garbage collector. It also describes how to control the amount of I/O operations that Elasticsearch uses for segment merging and to store modules.

Chapter 7, Snapshot and Restore, covers the Elasticsearch snapshot and restore module, how to define a snapshot repository, different repository types, the process of snapshot and restore, and how to configure them. It also describes how the snapshot process works.

Chapter 8, Improving the User Search Experience, introduces Elasticsearch suggesters, which allow us to correct spelling mistakes and build efficient autocomplete mechanisms. It also covers how to improve query relevance by using different Elasticsearch functionalities such as boosting and synonyms.

What you need for this book

You need a stable version of Elasticsearch. The code of the book is compatible with Elasticsearch version 1 and later. You can examine the code of the book using cURL (that is, Client URL Library) on Linux and MacOS X. Plus, if you need a user-friendly query interface, you can use the sense plugin running on Chrome (`https://chrome.google.com/webstore/detail/sense-beta/lhjgkmllcaadmopgmanpapmpjgmfcfig?hl=en`).

Who this book is for

If you understand the importance of a great search experience, this book will show you exactly how to build one with Elasticsearch—one of the world's leading search servers.

Conventions

In this book, you will find a number of text styles that distinguish between different kinds of information. Here are some examples of these styles and an explanation of their meaning.

Code words in text, database table names, folder names, filenames, file extensions, pathnames, dummy URLs, user input, and Twitter handles are shown as follows: "We can include other contexts through the use of the `include` directive."

A block of code is set as follows:

```
curl -XPOST localhost:9200/company/employee -d '{
  "firstname": "Joe Jeffers",
  "lastname": "Hoffman",
  "age": 30
}'
{"_index":"company","_type":"employee","_id":"AU7GIEQeR7spPlxvqlud","_version":1,"created":true}
```

Any command-line input or output is written as follows:

```
curl -XGET 'localhost:9200/_cat/health?pretty'
1448644024 19:07:04 elasticsearch yellow 1 1 6 6 0 0 6 0
```

New terms and **important words** are shown in bold. Words that you see on the screen, for example, in menus or dialog boxes, appear in the text like this: "Elasticsearch allows us to use the Suggest API functionality."

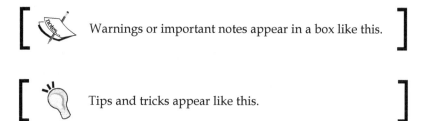

> Warnings or important notes appear in a box like this.

> Tips and tricks appear like this.

Reader feedback

Feedback from our readers is always welcome. Let us know what you think about this book—what you liked or disliked. Reader feedback is important for us as it helps us develop titles that you will really get the most out of.

To send us general feedback, simply e-mail `feedback@packtpub.com`, and mention the book's title in the subject of your message.

If there is a topic that you have expertise in and you are interested in either writing or contributing to a book, see our author guide at `www.packtpub.com/authors`.

Customer support

Now that you are the proud owner of a Packt book, we have a number of things to help you to get the most from your purchase.

Downloading the example code

You can download the example code files from your account at `http://www.packtpub.com` for all the Packt Publishing books you have purchased. If you purchased this book elsewhere, you can visit `http://www.packtpub.com/support` and register to have the files e-mailed directly to you.

Errata

Although we have taken every care to ensure the accuracy of our content, mistakes do happen. If you find a mistake in one of our books—maybe a mistake in the text or the code—we would be grateful if you could report this to us. By doing so, you can save other readers from frustration and help us improve subsequent versions of this book. If you find any errata, please report them by visiting `http://www.packtpub.com/submit-errata`, selecting your book, clicking on the **Errata Submission Form** link, and entering the details of your errata. Once your errata are verified, your submission will be accepted and the errata will be uploaded to our website or added to any list of existing errata under the Errata section of that title.

To view the previously submitted errata, go to `https://www.packtpub.com/books/content/support` and enter the name of the book in the search field. The required information will appear under the **Errata** section.

Piracy

Piracy of copyrighted material on the Internet is an ongoing problem across all media. At Packt, we take the protection of our copyright and licenses very seriously. If you come across any illegal copies of our works in any form on the Internet, please provide us with the location address or website name immediately so that we can pursue a remedy.

Please contact us at `copyright@packtpub.com` with a link to the suspected pirated material.

We appreciate your help in protecting our authors and our ability to bring you valuable content.

Questions

If you have a problem with any aspect of this book, you can contact us at `questions@packtpub.com`, and we will do our best to address the problem.

1
Introduction to Efficient Indexing

Elasticsearch is an open source **full text search** engine and data analysis tool that was developed in Java, is Apache Lucene-based, and scalable. A huge scale of data is produced at every moment in today's world of information technologies, in social media, in video sharing sites, and in medium and large-sized companies that provide services in communication, health, security, and other areas. Here we are talking about an information/data ocean, and we call this ocean briefly as **big data** in the world of information technology. An important part of this world of big data is unstructured, scattered, and insignificant when it is in isolation.

For this reason, some requirements such as recording, accessing, analyzing, and processing of data are significant. Like similar search engines, Elasticsearch is one of the tools that have been developed to deal with the problems mentioned previously, which belong to the world of big data.

What should I look for — high efficiency and/or performance — when Elasticsearch is used for the purposes mentioned earlier?

This book will target experienced developers who have used Elasticsearch before and want to extend their knowledge about how to effectively perform Elasticsearch indexing. Therefore, this book assumes that the reader already knows the basic issues and concepts of Elasticsearch. For example, what is Elasticsearch, how to install it, what purposes it serves, and so on. This book in your hand is intended to assist you with technical information and concrete applications about efficient indexing and relevant search result in Elasticsearch. This chapter aims to introduce and discuss the main topics for the purposes mentioned previously. To this end, we will look closely at how to store data by Elasticsearch and try to understand the document storage strategy. The relevant search result is closely related to data analysis. Hence, we will do an introduction to understanding the analysis process. In other chapters of this book, you will find the necessary discussions and examples for a better understanding of the following main issues:

- How to store documents
- The difference between the storable and searchable field
- What the function of the analyzer is
- How to improve relevant search results

Getting started

How does Elasticsearch store date and how does Elasticsearch store access data? These should be the first questions that come to mind when it comes to efficient indexing. The first thing to understand is how the documents are stored and accessed by Elasticsearch for efficient indexing and to improve the querying experience.

The purpose of this chapter is to prepare your mind for the topics that will be discussed throughout the book in more detail.

Understanding the document storage strategy

First of all, we need to depict the question: what is an Elasticsearch index?

The short answer is that an index is like a **database** in a relational database. Elasticsearch is a **document-oriented** search and analytics engine. Each record in Elasticsearch is a structured JSON document. In other words, each piece of data that is sent to Elasticsearch for indexing is a JSON document. All fields of the documents are indexed by default, and these indexed fields can be used in a single query. More information about this can be found in the next chapter.

Elasticsearch uses the **Apache Lucene** library for writing and reading the data from the index. In fact, Apache Lucene is at the heart of Elasticsearch.

 Apache Lucene is a high-performance, full-featured text search engine library written entirely in Java. If you want to more information, please refer to `https://lucene.apache.org/core/`.

Every document sent to Elasticsearch is stored in Apache Lucene and the library stores all data in a data structure called an **inverted index**. An inverted index is a data structure that is mapped documents and terms. That means that an inverted index has a list of all the unique words that appear in any document. Also, it has a list of documents in which the collected unique word appears. Intended with this data structure, the performance of fast full-text searching is performed at low cost. The inverted index is a basic indexing algorithm used by search engines.

 The inverted index will be discussed in depth in the next chapter.

The _source field

As mentioned earlier, all fields of the documents are indexed by default in Elasticsearch, and these fields can be used in a single query. We usually send data to Elasticsearch because we want to either search or retrieve them.

The _source field is a metadata field automatically generated during indexing within Lucene that stores the actual JSON document. **When executing search requests, the** _source **field is returned by default** as shown in the following code snippet:

```
curl -XPUT localhost:9200/my_index/article/1 -d '{
  "title": "What is an Elasticsearch Index",
  "category": "Elasticsearch",
  "content": "An index is like a...",
  "date": "2015-07-18",
  "tags": ["bigdata", "elasticsearch"]
}'
{"_index":"my_index","_type":"article","_id":"1","_
version":1,"created":true}

curl -XGET localhost:9200/my_index/_search?pretty
{
    "took": 2,
    "timed_out": false,
```

```
   "_shards": {
      "total": 5,
      "successful": 5,
      "failed": 0
   },
   "hits": {
      "total": 1,
      "max_score": 1,
      "hits": [
         {
            "_index": "my_index",
            "_type": "article",
            "_id": "1",
            "_score": 1,
            "_source": {
               "title": "What is an Elasticsearch Index",
               "category": "Elasticsearch",
               "content": "An index is like a...",
               "date": "2015-07-18",
               "tags": [
"bigdata",
"elasticsearch"
               ]
            }
         }
      ]
   }
}
```

 More information about the metadata fields can be found in *Chapter 3, Basic Concepts of Mapping*.

We sent a document to Elasticsearch that contains `title`, `category`, `content`, `date`, and `tags` fields for indexing. Then we ran the search command. The result of the search command is shown in the preceding snippet.

Because it is always able to return everything you send to Elasticsearch as a search result, **Elasticsearch stores every document field within the** `_source` **field by default**, which you send to it.

You can change this behavior if you want. This can be a preferred option because in some cases you may not need all fields to be returned in the search results. Also, it does not require a field to be stored in the _source field while it is searchable:

```
curl -XPUT localhost:9200/my_index/_mapping/article -d '{
   "article": {
     "_source": {
       "excludes": [
"date"
       ]
     }
   }
}'
{"acknowledged":true}

curl -XPUT localhost:9200/my_index/article/1 -d '{
   "title": "What is an Elasticsearch Index",
   "category": "Elasticsearch",
   "content": "An index is like a...",
   "date": "2015-07-18",
   "tags": ["bigdata", "elasticsearch"]
}'
{"_index":"my_index","_type":"article","_id":"1","_
version":2,"created":false}
```

What did we do?

Firstly, we removed the date field from the _source field by changing the dynamic mapping. Then we sent the same document to Elasticsearch again for reindexing. In the next step, we will try to list the records that are greater than or equal to July 18, 2015 using the range query. The pretty parameter used in the following query tells Elasticsearch to return pretty-printed JSON results:

```
curl -XGET localhost:9200/my_index/_search?pretty -d '{
   "query": {
     "range": {
       "date": {
         "gte": "2015-07-18"
       }
     }
   }
}'
{
    "took": 2,
    "timed_out": false,
```

```
    "_shards": {
        "total": 5,
        "successful": 5,
        "failed": 0
    },
    "hits": {
        "total": 1,
        "max_score": 1,
        "hits": [
            {
                "_index": "my_index",
                "_type": "article",
                "_id": "1",
                "_score": 1,
                "_source": {
                    "title": "What is an Elasticsearch Index",
                    "category": "Elasticsearch",
                    "content": "An index is like a...",
                    "tags": [
"bigdata",
"elasticsearch"
                    ]
                }
            }
        ]
    }
}
```

As you can see, we can search in the date field that although is not returned. This is because, as previously mentioned, all fields of the documents are indexed as default by Elasticsearch.

The difference between the storable and searchable field

Elasticsearch allows you to separately manage fields that can be searchable and/or storable. This is useful because in some cases we may want to index a field but may not want to store it or vice versa. In some cases, we might not want to do either.

On behalf of a better understanding of the subject, let's change the preceding example. Let's create the my_index again with the explicit mapping and disable the _source field:

```
curl -XDELETE localhost:9200/my_index
{"acknowledged": true}
```

```
curl -XPUT localhost:9200/my_index -d '{
  "mappings": {
    "article": {
      "_source": {
        "enabled": false
        },
      "properties": {
        "title": {"type": "string", "store": true},
        "category": {"type": "string"},
        "content": {"type": "string"},
        "date": {"type": "date", "index": "no"},
        "tags": {"type": "string", "index": "no", "store": true}
      }
    }
  }
}'
```

Firstly, we disabled the _source field for the article type. In this case, unless otherwise stated, any fields of the article type are not stored/returned. However, we would like to store some fields. In this case, we want to store only the title and tags fields using the store feature. If we enable the store option, we let Elasticsearch store the specified fields. Therefore, we explicitly specify which fields we want to store for future scenarios.

In addition, we don't want some fields to be indexed. This means that such fields will not be searchable. The date and the tags fields will not be searchable with the preceding configuration but, if requested, the tags field can be returned.

> Keep in mind that after disabling the _source field, you cannot make use of a number of features that come with the _source field, for example, the update API and highlighting.

Now, let's see the effect of the preceding configuration in practice:

```
curl -XPUT localhost:9200/my_index/article/1 -d '{
  "title": "What is an Elasticsearch Index",
  "category": "Elasticsearch",
  "content": "An index is like a...",
  "date": "2015-07-18",
  "tags": ["bigdata", "elasticsearch"]
}'
{"_index":"my_index","_type":"article","_id":"1","_
version":1,"created":true}

curl -XGET localhost:9200/my_index/_search?pretty
```

```
{
  "took" : 2,
  "timed_out" : false,
  "_shards" : {
    "total" : 5,
    "successful" : 5,
    "failed" : 0
  },
  "hits" : {
    "total" : 1,
    "max_score" : 1.0,
    "hits" : [ {
      "_index" : "my_index",
      "_type" : "article",
      "_id" : "1",
      "_score" : 1.0
    } ]
  }
}

curl -XGET localhost:9200/my_index/_search?pretty -d '{
  "query": {
    "range": {
      "date": {
        "gte": "2015-07-18"
      }
    }
  }
}'
{
  "took": 6,
  "timed_out": false,
  "_shards": {
    "total": 5,
    "successful": 5,
    "failed": 0
  },
  "hits": {
    "total": 0,
    "max_score": null,
    "hits": []
  }
}
```

Firstly, we sent a document containing the `date` field value that is `2015-07-18` for indexing, and we ran the `match_all` query after (*The search request does not have a body*) and we did not see the `_source` field within **hits**.

Then we ran a `range` query on the `date` field because we want the documents where the date is greater than and equal to July 18, 2015. Elasticsearch did not return any documents to us because the `date` field does not have a default configuration. In other words, the `date` field was not indexed, therefore not searchable, so we do not see any retrieved documents.

Now let's run another scenario with following command:

```
curl -XGET localhost:9200/my_index/_search?pretty -d '{
  "fields": ["title", "content", "tags"],
  "query": {
    "match": {
      "content": "like"
    }
  }
}'
{
    "took": 6,
    "timed_out": false,
    "_shards": {
       "total": 5,
       "successful": 5,
       "failed": 0
    },
    "hits": {
       "total": 1,
       "max_score": 0.13424811,
       "hits": [
          {
             "_index": "my_index",
             "_type": "article",
             "_id": "1",
             "_score": 0.13424811,
             "fields": {
                "title": [
"What is an Elasticsearch Index"
                ],
                "tags": [
"bigdata",
"elasticsearch"
```

```
                    ]
                }
            }
        ]
    }
}
```

The document is returned to us as a result of the preceding query because the content field is searchable; but the field is not returned because it was not stored in Lucene.

Understanding the difference between storable and searchable (*indexed*) fields is important for indexing performance and relevant search results. It offers significant advantages for high-level users.

Analysis

We mentioned earlier that all of Apache Lucene's data is stored in an inverted index. This transformation is required for successful response by Elasticsearch to search requests. **The process of transforming this data is called analysis**.

Elasticsearch has an index analysis module. It maps to the Lucene Analyzer. In general, analyzers are composed of a single Tokenizer and zero or more TokenFilters.

 Analysis modules and analyzers will be discussed in depth in *Chapter 4, Analysis and Analyzers*.

Elasticsearch provides a lot of character filters, tokenizers, and token filters. For example, a character filter may be used to strip out HTML markup and a token filter may be used to modify tokens (for example, *lowercase*). You can combine them to create custom analyzers or you can use its built-in analyzer.

Good understanding of the process of analysis is very important in terms of improving the user's search experience and relevant search results because **Elasticsearch (actually Lucene) will use analyzer during indexing and query time**.

 It is crucial to remember that all Elasticsearch queries are not being analyzed.

Now let's examine the importance of the analyzer in terms of relevant search results with a simple scenario:

```
curl -XPOST localhost:9200/company/employee -d '{
    "firstname": "Joe Jeffers",
```

```
    "lastname": "Hoffman",
    "age": 30
}'
{"_index":"company","_type":"employee","_id":"AU7GIEQeR7spPlxvqlud","_
version":1,"created":true}
```

We indexed an employee. His name is Joe Jeffers Hoffman, 30 years old. Let's search the employees that are named Joe in the company index now:

```
curl -XGET localhost:9200/company/_search?pretty -d '{
  "query": {
    "match": {
      "firstname": "joe"
    }
  }
}'
{
    "took": 68,
    "timed_out": false,
    "_shards": {
        "total": 5,
        "successful": 5,
        "failed": 0
    },
    "hits": {
        "total": 1,
        "max_score": 0.19178301,
        "hits": [
            {
                "_index": "company",
                "_type": "employee",
                "_id": "AU7GIEQeR7spPlxvqlud",
                "_score": 0.19178301,
                "_source": {
                    "firstname": "Joe Jeffers",
                    "lastname": "Hoffman",
                    "age": 30
                }
            }
        ]
    }
}
```

All string type fields in the company index will be analyzed by a standard analyzer because employee types were created with dynamic mapping.

The **standard analyzer** is the default analyzer that Elasticsearch uses. It removes most punctuation and splits the text on word boundaries, as defined by the **Unicode Consortium.**

 If you want to have more information about the Unicode Consortium, please refer to
`http://www.unicode.org/reports/tr29/`.

In this case, Joe Jeffers would be two tokens (Joe and Jeffers). To see how the standard analyzer works, run the following command:

```
curl -XGET 'localhost:9200/_analyze?analyzer=standard&pretty' -d 'Joe
Jeffers'
{
  "tokens" : [ {
    "token" : "joe",
    "start_offset" : 0,
    "end_offset" : 3,
    "type" : "<ALPHANUM>",
    "position" : 1
  }, {
    "token" : "jeffers",
    "start_offset" : 4,
    "end_offset" : 11,
    "type" : "<ALPHANUM>",
    "position" : 2
  } ]
}
```

We searched the letters joe and the consequent document containing Joe Jeffers was returned to us because the standard analyzer had split the text on word boundaries and converted to lowercase. The standard analyzer is built using the Lower Case Token Filter along with other filters (the *Standard Token Filter* and *Stop Token Filter,* for example).

Now let's examine the following example:

```
curl -XDELETE localhost:9200/company
{"acknowledged":true}

curl -XPUT localhost:9200/company -d '{
  "mappings": {
    "employee": {
      "properties": {
```

```
            "firstname": {"type": "string", "index": "not_analyzed"}
          }
        }
      }
}'
{"acknowledged":true}

curl -XPOST localhost:9200/company/employee -d '{
  "firstname": "Joe Jeffers",
  "lastname": "Hoffman",
  "age": 30
}'
{"_index":"company","_type":"employee","_id":"AU7GOF2wR7spPlxvqmHY","_
version":1,"created":true}
```

We deleted the company index created by dynamic mapping and recreated it with explicit mapping. This time, we used the not_analyzed value of the index option on the firstname field in the employee type. This means that the field is not analyzed at indexing time:

```
curl -XGET localhost:9200/company/_search?pretty -d '{
  "query": {
    "match": {
      "firstname": "joe"
    }
  }
}'
{
  "took": 12,
  "timed_out": false,
  "_shards": {
    "total": 5,
    "successful": 2,
    "failed": 0
  },
  "hits": {
    "total": 0,
    "max_score": null,
    "hits": []
  }
}
```

As you can see, Elasticsearch did not return a result to us with the match query because the `firstname` field is configured to the `not_analyzed` value. Therefore, Elasticsearch did not use an analyzer during indexing; the indexed value was exactly as specified. In other words, `Joe Jeffers` was a single token. Unless otherwise indicated, the match query uses the default search analyzer. Therefore, if you want a document to return to us with the match query without changing the analyzer in this example, we need to specify the exact value (*paying attention to uppercase/lowercase*):

```
curl -XGET localhost:9200/company/_search?pretty -d '{
  "query": {
    "match" : {
        "firstname": "Joe Jeffers"
    }
  }
}'
```

The preceding command will return us the document we searched for. Now let's examine the following example:

```
curl -XGET localhost:9200/company/_search?pretty -d '{
  "query": {
    "match_phrase_prefix": {
        "firstname": "Joe"
    }
  }
}'
{
   "took": 2,
   "timed_out": false,
   "_shards": {
      "total": 5,
      "successful": 5,****
      "failed": 0
   },
   "hits": {
      "total": 1,
      "max_score": 0.30685282,
      "hits": [
         {
            "_index": "company",
            "_type": "employee",
            "_id": "AU7GOF2wR7spPlxvqmHY",
            "_score": 0.30685282,
            "_source": {
```

```
            "firstname": "Joe Jeffers",
            "lastname": "Hoffman",
            "age": 30
          }
        }
      ]
    }
  }
}
```

As you can see, our searched document was returned to us although we did not specify the exact value (*please note that we still use uppercase letters*) because the match_ phrase_prefix query analyzes the text and creates a phrase query out of the analyzed text. It allows for prefix matches on the last term in the text.

Summary

In this chapter, we' looked at the important, main topics for efficient indexing and relevant search results: How to store documents? What is the difference between the storable and searchable field? What is the analysis process? What is the impact on the relevant search results? In addition to that, we've briefly discussed some of the basic concepts of Elasticsearch that are associated with Lucene (for example, inverted index and the _source field).

In the next chapter, you'll learn about the Elasticsearch index—what mapping is, what inverted index is, the denormalized data structure—and some other concepts related to this topic.

2
What is an Elasticsearch Index

In the previous chapter, we looked at what the difference is when a field becomes indexed and searchable and at how the analysis process affects the relevant search results. In this chapter, we will dive deep into the concept of the Elasticsearch index. Therefore, we will first go through basic concepts. Then we will examine the inverted index data structure. By the end of this chapter, we will have covered the following topics:

- What is dynamic mapping?
- What is denormalization?
- Is index flexible?
- What is the inverted index?

Nature of the Elasticsearch index

Let's go through the basic concepts of Elasticsearch indices and their features.

Indices

Elasticsearch is **document-oriented**. Each record in Elasticsearch is a document. Elasticsearch uses **JSON (JavaScript Object Notation)** as the serialization format for documents. Therefore, each piece of data that is sent to Elasticsearch for indexing is a JSON document.

 JSON is an open standard format that uses human-readable text to transmit data objects consisting of attribute–value pairs. If you want more information, please refer to `https://en.wikipedia.org/wiki/JSON`.

Elasticsearch indices compared to **database management systems** may be considered to be databases. **How a database is a collection of regular information, Elasticsearch indices are a collection of structured JSON document**. In other words, an index is a logical partition for user data.

Documents are stored in the same index of similar characteristics, for example, your member data in the member index, your customer data in the customer index, and so on. In this sense, the index names refer to grouped documents. Like in SQL world, a database name refers to a regular collection of information.

As mentioned in the previous chapter, Elasticsearch uses the **Apache Lucene** library for writing and reading the data from the index. Apache Lucene stores all data in a data structure called an **inverted index**. An inverted index is a data structure mapped to documents and terms. We will examine the Inverted Index data structure in detail after discussing the basic concepts.

When it comes to indices, we need to talk about the data distribution mechanism used by Elasticsearch. Elasticsearch uses shards and replicas in order to distribute data around the cluster.

Elasticsearch distributes data to more than one Lucene index as physical by default. These indices are called **shards** and this distribution process is called **sharding**. A shard is automatically managed by Elasticsearch. It is a low-level worker unit. Take a look at the following distribution strategy:

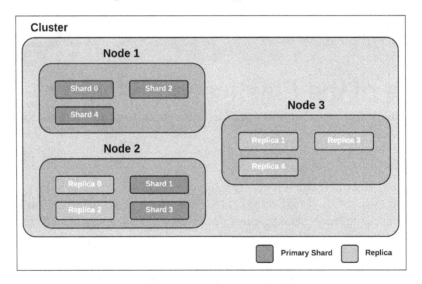

Understanding the distribution strategy of Elasticsearch is important in the context of efficient indexing, and this topic will be dealt with in greater detail in *Chapter 5, Anatomy of an Elasticsearch Cluster* with shards and replicas.

Mapping

When trying to understand the nature of Elasticsearch index, we need to look closely at the concept of mapping.

Mapping is the process of defining how a document should be indexed to Elasticsearch. In addition to this, how to analyze the fields of the target query is determined by mapping.

Types are created according to the mapping information. It is important to know that Elasticsearch creates mapping automatically based on the data sent. When data is added, Elasticsearch tries to identify the data structure and makes it searchable. This process is known as *dynamic mapping*.

Mapping is very important for relevant search results, and from this point it should be understood quite well that how a field is analyzed is determined by mapping.

 Mapping will be discussed with the basic concepts in the next chapter.

Types

Elasticsearch indices contain one or more type(s). Types can be considered as tables, again compared to database management systems. Types ensure grouped documents under indices like tables do.

It is important to understand that although documents are grouped with similar characteristics under indices and types, **Elasticsearch is not limiting in our search to a particular index or type**:

```
curl -XGET localhost:9200/ purchaser,vendor/_search -d '{
  "query": {
    "match": {
      "country": "Turkey"
    }
  }
}'
```

In the preceding example, we have searched across all documents in the `purchaser` and `vendor` indices without specifying the type:

```
curl -XGET localhost:9200/publisher/author,reviewer/_search -d '{
  "query": {
    "match": {
```

```
       "city": "İstanbul"
     }
   }
 }'
```

This time we have searched across all documents in the `author` and `reviewer` types of the `publisher` index.

Document

In the Elasticsearch world (that is, *in Lucene world*), a document is the main entity and basic unit of user data.

As mentioned earlier, the document format is JSON. Documents consist of fields (that is, *properties*) and value pairs. Each field has a name and a type supporting existing data types. A field is stored physically in a type within an index as an element of a document that has a unique ID.

Now, let's send a document to Elasticsearch:

```
curl -XPOST localhost:9200/premierleague/topscorer -d '{
  "fullname": "Robin van Persie",
  "age": 32,
  "birthdate": "1983-08-06",
 "current_club": "Fenerbahce SK"
 }'
{"_index":"premierleague","_type":"topscorer","_
id":"AU8I47O90qdql2fUT1Oh","_version":1,"created":true}
```

As seen, we indexed the document without any preparation. Because Elasticsearch is *schema-less*, it does not request some definitions such as index, type, and field type before the indexing process.

 We'll discuss the question, "Is the claim about 'Elasticsearch stands for the schema-free model' always true?" in the next chapter.

The following command shows us the mapping for the fields that Elasticsearch generated dynamically from the documents that we indexed:

```
curl -XGET localhost:9200/premierleague/_mapping/topscorer?pretty
{
  "premierleague" : {
    "mappings" : {
      "topscorer" : {
```

```
        "properties" : {
          "current_club": {
            "type": "string"
          },
          "age" : {
            "type" : "long"
          },
          "birthdate" : {
            "type" : "date",
            "format" : "dateOptionalTime"
          },
          "fullname" : {
            "type" : "string"
          }
        }
      }
    }
  }
}
```

Documents do not necessarily have similar fields and data structures. For example, a document with string values (in fields) and another document containing long/date values (of fields) can be both stored in the same type. Containing documents that have fields with different types, names, and different number of in the same index is undoubtedly valuable. This also means that an object can be indexed later with a new property and will automatically be added to the mapping definitions. **It is important to understand that flexibility is provided by Elasticsearch**. This situation can be likened to table and column independence that is provided by *NoSQL* architectures. This also means that you can easily *denormalize* your data.

Denormalization

Denormalization is the process of optimizing the read performance of a database by adding redundant data. A normalized design often stores related pieces of information in separate logical tables. Consequently, in this case, we will be performing the expensive join operations at which most NoSQL system are poor. In most cases, when you deal with unstructured data, you must consider the denormalized model for your data because, while the normalization model provides a fixed-schema model, the denormalized model relies on schema-free data.

You sometimes need to denormalize your data because the advantage of data denormalization is speed. Now let's examine the following example:

```
curl -XPUT localhost:9200/my_index/author/1 -d '{
  "name": "David Karp",
  "email": "david@karp.com",
  "dob": "1986/07/06"
}'
{"_index":"my_index","_type":"author","_id":"1","_
version":1,"created":true}

curl -XPUT localhost:9200/my_index/article/1 -d '{
  "title":     "Story on Tumblr",
  "body":      "This story is...",
  "user":      {
    "id":       1,
    "name":     "David Karp"
  }
}'
{"_index":"my_index","_type":"article","_id":"1","_
version":1,"created":true}
```

Part of the author's data has been denormalized into the preceding article document. In this way, we can find articles about relationships by the author called David with a single query:

```
Curl -XGET localhost:9200/my_index/article/_search?pretty -d '{
  "query": {
    "bool": {
      "must": [
        { "match":
          {"title":"tumblr" }
        },
        { "match":
          { "user.name": "David" }
        }
      ]
    }
  }
}'
```

In this structure, each document contains all of the information; thus, there is no need to join operations.

Inverted index

As mentioned in the previous chapter, Elasticsearch uses **Apache Lucene**, which stores all data in a data structure called an inverted index. An inverted index is an index data structure that is designed to allow very fast **full-text searches**. In this data structure are mapped terms (*unique words*) and documents. This is such that an inverted index consists of a list of all the unique words, and for each word, a list of the documents.

To better understand an inverted index, let's examine a scenario in which we have three documents. These documents include the `title` and `tags` fields. If you run the `match_all` query on the type that contains the documents, you will see the following response:

```
{
            "_index": "my_index",
            "_type": "article",
            "_id": "1",
            "_score": 1,
            "_source": {
                "title": "core spring",
                "tags": [
"java",
"spring"
                ]
            }
        },
        {
            "_index": "my_index",
            "_type": "article",
            "_id": "2",
            "_score": 1,
            "_source": {
                "title": "spring data",
                "tags": [
"java",
"bigdata"
                ]
            }
        },
        {
            "_index": "my_index",
            "_type": "article",
            "_id": "3",
            "_score": 1,
```

```
        "_source": {
            "title": "mongodb",
            "tags": [
"nosql",
"bigdata"
            ]
        }
    }
```

In such a scenario, Lucene first splits the fields of each document into separate words (that is, *terms or tokens*) and creates a list of all the unique terms and documents to store in the inverted index data structure.

The result is similar to the following figure:

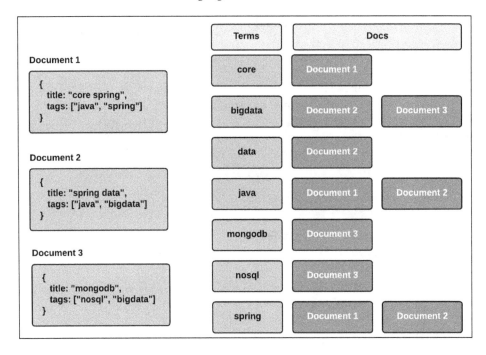

As you see, each unique term mapped with a document or documents. This structure allows an efficient and fast search, especially for term-based queries. The reason for this is clear: listing the documents per word is less expensive than listing the words per document in terms of system resources. In addition, an inverted index includes the position of each term within the document and has a numerical value indicating the incidence of a term. More simply, it looks something like the following:

Term	Count	Doc_1	Doc_2	Doc_3
core	1	x		
bigdata	2		x	x
data	1		x	
java	2	x	x	
mongodb	1			x
nosql	1			x
spring	2	x	x	

Each indexed field has a dedicated inverted index for fast retrieval in Lucene. It allows getting all the tokens for that particular field. At this point, this is very important: **an inverted index of a document and the actual document storage are two different things**. We discussed the difference between the storable and searchable field in the previous chapter. Inverted index is about being searchable but storage is related to the actual document and retrieving it (if you don't recall, please refer to *The difference between the storable and searchable field* section in the previous chapter).

Of course, a lot more can be said about the inverted index. But the first and most important thing you need to know is how the data is organized and we have talked about that enough.

Summary

In this chapter, we looked at the nature of the Elasticsearch index and reviewed the basic concepts: what dynamic mapping is, what it means, flexibility in the index, and what the inverted index is.

In the next chapter, you'll learn about the basic mapping concept: what basic mapping is, what the relationship between mapping and relevant search results is, Is the claim about 'Elasticsearch stands for the schema-free model' always true?, and some other subjects related to this topic.

3
Basic Concepts of Mapping

In the previous chapter, we talked about the nature of the Elasticsearch index. We started by looking at the basic concept and we discussed mapping. We talked about index flexibility and data denormalization. Finally, we discussed about inverted index and how the data is organized in an inverted index. In this chapter, we will continue to discuss mapping. We will first go through basic concepts. Then we'll focus on the relationship between mapping and relevant search results. Lastly, we will try to have a good grasp on schema-less. At the end of this chapter, we will have covered the following topics:

- What are metadata fields?
- How to control document metadata?
- What data types are?
- The relationship between mapping and getting relevant search results
- What is the meaning of schema-less?

Basic concepts and definitions

As stated in the previous chapter, mapping is the process of defining how a document should be mapped to Elasticsearch (if you don't recall, please refer to the *Mapping* section in the previous chapter). How a field is tokenized, analyzed, and searchable can be found using the mapping mechanism. Keep in mind that **mapping is actually a schema definition** (we will examine it in detail at the end of this chapter).

Now let's review the basic concepts and definitions.

Metadata fields

All the fields are not returned to us when a document is requested but each document has auto-generated *metadata fields* with each mapping which have information about the document that allows us to control how the metadata document is indexed. For example, which fields will return with the query results, how long the document will live, and so on.

We will now examine some of those fields.

_source

We have already talked at length about the _source field in *Chapter 1, Introduction to Efficient Indexing*; if you don't recall, please refer to the *_source* field section in the same chapter.

_all

Elasticsearch is a *full-text search* engine. It allows you to search in all fields of a document. This facility is provided by the _all field because it includes the text of one or more other fields within the document indexed and concatenates them into one big string. By default, the _all field is enabled and all fields are included in it for ease of use. You can exclude or include a field in the _all field with explicit field mappings and object mappings.

Now let's examine the following example:

```
curl -XPUT localhost:9200/my_index -d '{
  "mappings": {
    "employee": {
      "properties": {
        "firstname": { "type": "string" },
        "lastname": { "type": "string" },
        "addres": { "type": "string" },
        "phone": { "type": "string" },
        "email": { "type": "string" },
        "emailverification": {
          "type": "string" ,
          "include_in_all": false
        }
      }
    }
  }
}'
{"acknowledged":true}
```

The `emailverification` field was configured so as not to be stored in the `_all` field because we expect this field to have similar content like the email field and, hence, we do not want any extra storage costs:

```
curl -XPOST localhost:9200/my_index/employee -d '{
  "firstname": "Yuri",
  "lastname": "Zhirkov",
  "addres": "Moscow",
  "email": "info@yurizhirkov.com",
  "emailverification": "FC Dynamo Moscow"
}'
{"_index":"my_index","_type":"employee","_
id":"AU8o2KINuve3OHeb7oPu","_version":1,"created":true}

curl -XGET localhost:9200/my_index/employee/_search?pretty -d '{
  "query": {
    "match": {
      "_all": "dynamo"
    }
  }
}'
{
    "took": 1,
    "timed_out": false,
    "_shards": {
       "total": 5,
       "successful": 5,
       "failed": 0
    },
    "hits": {
       "total": 0,
       "max_score": null,
       "hits": []
    }
}
```

As you see, none of the documents were not returned to us when we searched the `dynamo` phrase in the `_all` field because this phrase was taking place in the `emailverification` field, which we already excluded in the `_all` field.

The `_all` field is very handy when we want to execute a search query against all the fields of a document, and also the use of extra disk space for fields that normally should not be the subject of a query may cause a waste of resources in terms of I/O operations as the preceding example illustrates.

What is essential to note (remember) is that this process comes at the expense of CPU cycles and index size.

 Keep in mind that the _all field is of the string type. This means that field values of different types are stored as a string type.

_timestamp

The _timestamp field provides a timestamp for a document. By default, it is disabled and is not stored. In order to enable and retrieve it, the following mapping should be defined:

```
curl -XPUT localhost:9200/my_index -d '{
   "mappings": {
     "employee": {
       "_timestamp" : {
              "enabled" : true,
              "store": true
          }
       }
     }
   }'
```

The _timestamp field can be queried as a standard date field and its value can be provided as an external value when indexing. In addition, it can also be automatically extracted from the document to index based on a path:

```
curl -XDELETE localhost:9200/my_index
{"acknowledged":true}

curl -XPUT localhost:9200/my_index -d '{
   "mappings": {
     "employee": {
       "_timestamp" : {
              "enabled" : true,
              "path" : "post_date",
              "store": true
          },
        "properties": {
          "firstname": { "type": "string" },
          "lastname": { "type": "string" },
          "addres": { "type": "string" },
          "phone": { "type": "string" },
          "email": { "type": "string" },
```

```
        "emailverification": {
          "type": "string" ,
          "include_in_all": false
        }
      }
    }
  }
}'
{"acknowledged":true}

curl -XPOST localhost:9200/my_index/employee -d '{
  "firstname": "Yuri",
  "lastname": "Zhirkov",
  "addres": "Moscow",
  "email": "info@yurizhirkov.com",
  "emailverification": "info@yurizhirkov.com",
  "post_date": "2013-11-15T14:12:12"
}'
{"_index":"my_index","_type":"employee","_
id":"AU8xYHKBrFAX9jIdDUds","_version":1,"created":true}
```

Okay, now we will request the saved document along with the `_timestamp` field:

```
curl -XGET my_index/employee/_search?pretty -d '{
  "fields": ["_timestamp", "_source"],
  "query": {
    "filtered": {
      "query": {
        "match_all": {}
      },
      "filter": {
        "range": {
          "_timestamp": {
            "gt" : "2013-11-15T00:00:00",
            "lt" : "2014-11-14T23:59:59"
          }
        }
      }
    }
  }
}'
{
    "took": 3,
    "timed_out": false,
    "_shards": {
```

```
          "total": 5,
          "successful": 5,
          "failed": 0
     },
     "hits": {
          "total": 1,
          "max_score": 1,
          "hits": [
               {
                    "_index": "my_index",
                    "_type": "employee",
                    "_id": "AU8xYHKBrFAX9jIdDUds",
                    "_score": 1,
                    "_source": {
                         "firstname": "Yuri",
                         "lastname": "Zhirkov",
                         "addres": "Moscow",
                         "email": "info@yurizhirkov.com",
                         "emailverification": "info@yurizhirkov.com",
                         "post_date": "2013-11-15T14:12:12"
                    },
                    "fields": {
                         "_timestamp": 1384524732000
                    }
               }
          ]
     }
}
```

It is important to note about the preceding example that was queried the
_timestamp field.

_ttl

This field allows you to set your documents to *time to live*. That will cause the expired
documents to be deleted automatically. It comes to disabled by default. In order to
enable it, the following mapping should be defined:

```
curl -XPUT localhost:9200/my_index -d '{
   "mappings": {
     "reminder": {
       "_ttl": {
         "enabled": true,
         "default" : "5m"
       }
```

```
      }
    }
  }'
{"acknowledged":true}
```

 Keep in mind that once _ttl is enabled, it is not allowed to be disabled.

In the preceding example, we enabled _ttl and we provide a default _ttl value, which is 5 minutes per index/type with the default feature. If you do not give a _ttl value, the document will never expire.

If you provide a ttl value at a document level, it will override the default value for the index. You can provide a _ttl value per document as follows:

```
curl -XPOST localhost:9200/my_index/reminder -d '{
  "user_id": 314,
  "temporary_password": "kj8nqw0xph",
  "_ttl": "30s"
}'
{"_index":"my_index","_type":"reminder","_
id":"AU82c07kRPPilXQ4LS16","_version":1,"created":true}
```

Types

One of the most important issues when configuring an index is that the document field must be configured with the appropriate data type. The type mapping allows us to control the data type of each field in a document. Now let's examine some types of other than the core types.

Object type

A JSON document can contain inner objects. When such a document is sent, Elasticsearch completely understands the nature of those inner objects and makes them searchable, for example, as follows:

```
curl -XPOST localhost:9200/my_index/department -d '{
  "computing": {
    "person": {
      "name": {
        "firstname": "Martin",
        "lastname": "Fowler"
      }
```

```
        }
      }
}'
{"_index":"my_index","_type":"department","_id":"AU84K4PGEOfq-
PnkfR_e","_version":1,"created":true}

curl -XGET localhost:9200/my_index/department/_search?pretty -d '{
   "query": {
     "match": {
        "computing.person.name.firstname": "martin"
     }
   }
}'
{
    "took": 4,
    "timed_out": false,
    "_shards": {
       "total": 5,
       "successful": 5,
       "failed": 0
    },
    "hits": {
       "total": 1,
       "max_score": 1,
       "hits": [
          {
             "_index": "my_index",
             "_type": "department",
             "_id": "AU84K4PGEOfq-PnkfR_e",
             "_score": 1,
             "_source": {
                "computing": {
                   "person": {
                      "name": {
                         "firstname": "Martin",
                         "lastname": "Fowler"
                      }
                   }
                }
             }
          }
       ]
    }
}
```

As you see, the inner object was successfully indexed because dynamic mapping is enabled by default in Elasticsearch. Please note the dot notation in the preceding command. We use the dot notation when we want to access an inner object or inner object field. For instance, in the preceding example, dot notation in the `computing.person` phrase refers to the person object, the next notation refers to name object, and the last notation refers to `firstname` field. In some cases, you might want to turn dynamic mapping off for inner objects. This can be very useful if you do not want *malformed objects*, which are an incompatible data type or format:

```
curl -XDELETE localhost:9200/my_index
{"acknowledged":true}

curl -XPUT localhost:9200/my_index -d '{
   "mappings": {
     "department": {
        "properties": {
            "computing": {
               "type": "object",
                "properties": {
                  "person": {
                    "properties": {
                      "name": {
                        "dynamic": false,
                        "properties": {
                          "firstname": {"type" : "string"},
                          "lastname": {"type" : "string"}
                        }
                      }
                    }
                  }
                }
            }
        }
     }
   }
}'
{"acknowledged":true}
```

In the preceding example, the name object mapped was configured by setting the dynamic property's value to `false`. This means that if we try to index with a new field within the name object, it will get discarded and will not be added to the mapping definition.

Let's see another example:

```
curl -XPOST localhost:9200/my_index/department -d '{
   "computing": {
      "person": {
         "name": {
            "firstname": "Martin",
            "lastname": "Fowler",
            "nickname": "martin"
         }
      }
   }
}'
{"_index":"my_index","_type":"department","_
id":"AU841UKxrec4gFOXhgdP","_version":1,"created":true}

curl -XGET localhost:9200/my_index/department/_mapping?pretty
{
   "my_index" : {
      "mappings" : {
         "department" : {
            "properties" : {
               "computing" : {
                  "properties" : {
                     "person" : {
                        "properties" : {
                           "name" : {
                              "dynamic" : "false",
                              "properties" : {
                                 "first_name" : {
                                    "type" : "string"
                                 },
                                 "last_name" : {
                                    "type" : "string"
                                 }
                              }
                           }
                        }
                     }
                  }
               }
            }
         }
      }
   }
}
```

The new field (`nickname`) did not cause a mapping to be updated, but it was indexed. So, if we ask Elasticsearch for the department type mapping, we see that it does not add a schema definition of the `nickname` field. However, the `nickname` field was indexed. This means that the `nickname` field will be returned to us when the document is requested. However, if we do not want it, we should set the dynamic parameter to strict `false` instead.

Root object type

The root object provides a type level configuration for fields such that it will be used in all fields, unless otherwise noted. For example, you can explicitly define both the `index_analyzer` and the `search_analyzer` parameters and specify a number of formats for date fields that will be added dynamically to your document as follows:

```
curl -XPUT localhost:9200/library -d '{
  "mappings": {
    "book" : {
      "index_analyzer" : "standard",
      "search_analyzer" : "standard",
      "dynamic_date_formats" : ["yyyy-MM-dd", "dd-MM-yyyy"],
      "properties" : {
        "title": {"type": "string"},
        "author": {"type": "string"},
        "editor": {"type": "string"},
        "isbn": {"type": "string"}
      }
    }
  }
}'
{"acknowledged":true}

curl -XPOST localhost:9200/library/book -d '{
  "title": "The Rumi Collection: An Anthology of Translations of
Mevlana Jalaluddin Rumi",
  "author": "Jelaluddin Rumi",
  "editor": "Kabir Helminski",
  "isbn": " 1570627177",
  "edition": "19-12-2000"
}'
{"_index":"library","_type":"book","_id":"AU8976hagyuvzb298bjq","_
version":1,"created":true}
```

 Keep in mind that `dynamic_date_formats` are not used for date fields that you specify in your mapping.

Attachment type

The attachment type allows indexing at a field **encoded as base64**. *HTML, ePub, Microsoft Office formats,* and so on can be considered to be indexed. The type is provided as a plugin extension. Please look at the plugin's README file for more information, available at: `https://github.com/elastic/elasticsearch-mapper-attachments`.

The relationship between mapping and relevant search results

It should be understood that how to store documents, control document metadata, data type of a field answer to questions, and so on, is through mapping. Similarly, as stated at the beginning of this chapter, using the mapping mechanism, we have answered how does mapping tokenize a field and analyze the field, it going to be searchable answers to questions, and so on, is also given by the mapping.

Now try to examine this situation closely through a simple scenario. Let's start with indexing that looks as follows:

```
curl -XPOST localhost:9200/blog/article -d '{"title":"HTML In
troduction","category":["HTML"],"content":"HTML is a markup
language for describing web documents...","publishdate":"10-01-
2013","tags":["html","markup-language"]}'

curl -XPOST localhost:9200/blog/article -d '{"title":"NoSQL
Concept and MongoDB","category":["NoSQL","BigData"],"content
":"In recent years, we often hear the name of NoSQL as a new
star...","publishdate":"14-06-2013","tags":["nosql","bigdata","mongo
db"]}'

curl -XPOST localhost:9200/blog/article -d '{"title":"NoSQL with JPA",
"category":["NoSQL","BigData","JPA"],"content":"EclipseLink, reference
implementation of JPA...","publishdate":"05-08-2013","tags":["nosql","
bigdata","mongodb","eclipselink","jpa"]}'

curl -XPOST localhost:9200/blog/article -d '{"title":"JSF 2.2: HTML
5 Support","category":["HTML","Java","JSF"],"content":"HTML 5 is the
fifth version of the HTML markup Standard...","publishdate":"21-08-
2013","tags":["html 5","jsf"]}'

curl -XPOST localhost:9200/blog/article -d '{"title":"Introduction to
ElasticSearch","category":["Java","BigData"],"content":"Elasticsearch
is an open source...","publishdate":"16-09-2013","tags":["java","bigda
ta","elasticsearch","search-engine"]}'
```

We indexed our personal blog that published five articles for search and analysis operations. Now, let's search for the Html 5 tag in the blog index:

```
curl -XGET localhost:9200/blog/_search?pretty -d '{
  "query": {
    "match": {
      "tags": "html 5"
    }
  }
}'
{
  "took": 36,
  "timed_out": false,
  "_shards": {
    "total": 5,
    "successful": 5,
    "failed": 0
  },
  "hits": {
    "total": 2,
    "max_score": 0.2169777,
    "hits": [
      {
        "_index": "blog",
        "_type": "article",
        "_id": "AU9Cb10ZT3fsfK8Z_ALA",
        "_score": 0.2169777,
        "_source": {
          "title": "JSF 2.2: HTML 5 Support",
          "category": [
            "HTML",
            "Java",
            "JSF"
          ],
          "content": "HTML 5 is the fifth version of the HTML
markup Standard...",
          "publishdate": "21-08-2013",
          "tags": [
            "html 5",
            "jsf"
          ]
        }
      },
      {
```

```
        "_index": "blog",
        "_type": "article",
        "_id": "AU9Cb1yxT3fsfK8Z_AK9",
        "_score": 0.02250402,
        "_source": {
            "title": "HTML Introduction",
            "category": [
                "HTML"
            ],
            "content": "HTML is a markup language for describing
web documents...",
            "publishdate": "10-01-2013",
            "tags": [
                "html",
                "markup-language"
            ]
        }
      }
    ]
  }
}
```

Oops, we have a problem.

Actually, we have a single document that contains HTML tag but two documents are returned by the query. The reason for this is that the Blog index was created with dynamic mapping. For this reason, the tags fields were analyzed by the standard analyzer. It removes most punctuation and splits the text on word boundaries, as defined by the Unicode Consortium. In this case, for example, the html 5 phrase is two tokens [html, 5]. Therefore, the html phrase matches with two documents that are containing the html and html 5 phrases in search time.

Now let's request intervals of a month in our articles using date histogram aggregation:

```
curl -XGET localhost:9200/blog/_search?pretty -d '{
  "size": 0,
  "aggs" : {
      "articles_over_time" : {
          "date_histogram" : {
              "field" : "publishdate",
              "interval" : "month"
          }
      }
  }
}
```

```
}'
{
    "error": "SearchPhaseExecutionException[Failed to execute phase
[query], all shards failed; shardFailures {[U2m824TnSbmOAnDZSjY5-A]
[blog][0]: ClassCastException[org.elasticsearch.index.fielddata.plain.
PagedBytesIndexFieldData cannot be cast to org.elasticsearch.index.
fielddata.IndexNumericFieldData]}{[U2m824TnSbmOAnDZSjY5-A][blog]
[1]: ClassCastException[org.elasticsearch.index.fielddata.plain.
PagedBytesIndexFieldData cannot be cast to org.elasticsearch.index.
fielddata.IndexNumericFieldData]}{[U2m824TnSbmOAnDZSjY5-A][blog]
[2]: ClassCastException[org.elasticsearch.index.fielddata.plain.
PagedBytesIndexFieldData cannot be cast to org.elasticsearch.index.
fielddata.IndexNumericFieldData]}{[U2m824TnSbmOAnDZSjY5-A][blog]
[3]: ClassCastException[org.elasticsearch.index.fielddata.plain.
PagedBytesIndexFieldData cannot be cast to org.elasticsearch.index.
fielddata.IndexNumericFieldData]}{[U2m824TnSbmOAnDZSjY5-A][blog]
[4]: ClassCastException[org.elasticsearch.index.fielddata.plain.
PagedBytesIndexFieldData cannot be cast to org.elasticsearch.index.
fielddata.IndexNumericFieldData]}]",
    "status": 500
}
```

Oops, we have a bigger problem now than ever.

Date histogram aggregation can only be applied on date values. This is the source of our problem. Now let's request the mapping details of the article type in the blog index:

```
curl -XGET localhost:9200/blog/article/_mapping?pretty
This gives us the following mapping detail:
{
    "blog": {
        "mappings": {
            "article": {
                "properties": {
                    "category": {
                        "type": "string"
                    },
                    "content": {
                        "type": "string"
                    },
                    "publishdate": {
                        "type": "string"
                    },
                    "tags": {
                        "type": "string"
                    },
```

```
                    "title": {
                        "type": "string"
                    }
                }
            }
        }
    }
}
```

As you can see, the `publishdate` field is of type string. Elasticsearch uses **Joda** for parsing dates. The default date parsing technique is *ISODateTimeFormat. dateOptionalTimeParser*. That creates instances of DateTimeFormatter based on the ISO8601 standard.

 If you want more information about Joda, please refer to `http://www.joda.org/joda-time/`.

As mentioned previously, the Blog index was created with dynamic mapping. For this reason, the `publishdate` field has been recognized as a field of type `string` by Elasticsearch because the value of the field is incompatible with the default date format.

Now, the blog index must consider our needs; let's recreate the `blog` index with explicit mapping.

Our needs:

1. We want to search by an exact value from the `tag` field.
2. We want to use the date query (as a date histogram aggregation) on the `date` field.

Let's look at the following snippet:

```
curl -XDELETE localhost:9200/blog
{"acknowledged":true}

curl -XPUT localhost:9200/blog -d '{
    "mappings": {
        "article" : {
            "properties" : {
                "title": {"type": "string"},
                "category": {"type": "string"},
                "content": {"type": "string"},
                "publishdate": {"type": "date", "format": "dd-MM-yyyy"},
```

```
            "tags": {"type": "string", "index": "not_analyzed"}
        }
    }
}
}'
{"acknowledged":true}
```

In the preceding explicit mapping, firstly, we defined the date format for the `publishdate` field and then we used the `not_analyzed` value of the index option on the `tags` field. This means the `tags` field is not analyzed at indexing time. So, the indexed field's value was exactly as specified. In other words, "html 5" phrase will be a single token.

Now we are able to get the results we expect from the queries after running.

Understanding the schema-less

Certainly one of the most important features of Elasticsearch is its ability to be schema-less but it must be digested with no doubt.

Yes, as stated previously, Elasticsearch does not require some definitions such as index, type, and field type before the indexing process, and when an object is indexed later with a new property, it will automatically be added to the mapping definitions.

So, is the claim about "Elasticsearch stands for the schema-free model" always true?

Recall that **types are being created according to the mapping information and mapping is actually a schema definition**. Therefore, Elasticsearch expects that mapping and the documents being indexed are compatible.

Now let's examine the following example:

```
curl -XPUT localhost:9200/my_index/document/1 -d '{"value": "a"}'
{"_index":"my_index","_type":"document","_id":"1","_
version":1,"created":true}

curl -XPUT localhost:9200/my_index/document/2 -d '{"value": 1}'
{"_index":"my_index","_type":"document","_id":"2","_
version":1,"created":true}
```

Everything seems fine. Let's now request mapping for the document type. This gives us the following result:

```
curl -XGET localhost:9200/my_index/document/_mapping?pretty
{
  "my_index" : {
```

```
        "mappings" : {
          "document" : {
            "properties" : {
              "value" : {
                "type" : "string"
              }
            }
          }
        }
      }
    }
  }
}
```

The response shows that the value field has been recognized as a field of type string by Elasticsearch because the first value being a string value (that is, a) was sent (*remember, explicit mapping was used*). In this case, when the second document was indexed, Elasticsearch converted the numeric value into a string value.

Okay, now we will delete the my_index and indexing the documents in reverse order:

```
curl -XDELETE localhost:9200/my_index
{"acknowledged":true}

curl -XPUT localhost:9200/my_index/document/1 -d '{"value": 1}'
{"_index":"my_index","_type":"document","_id":"1","_
version":1,"created":true}
```

So far so good. Let's continue:

```
curl -XPUT localhost:9200/my_index/document/2 -d '{"value": "a"}'
{"error":"MapperParsingException[failed to parse [value]]; nested:
NumberFormatException[For input string: \"a\"]; ","status":400}
```

Oops, we have a big problem. As you seen, the server returns a **400 Bad Request** when we submit the second document. Let's now again request mapping for the document type:

```
curl -XGET localhost:9200/my_index/document/_mapping?pretty
{
  "my_index" : {
    "mappings" : {
      "document" : {
        "properties" : {
          "value" : {
            "type" : "long"
          }
```

```
          }
        }
      }
    }
  }
```

As you can see, the `value` field has been recognized as a field of type long by Elasticsearch because the first value being a numeric value (that is, 1) was sent (*remember again, explicit mapping was used*). In this case, when the second document was indexed, *Elasticsearch tried to parse the string value* a *as a numeric value* and threw a `NumberFormatException` as this string can't be parsed numerically.

We cannot solve this problem by deleting the first document because this action does not change the mapping information. Keep in mind that **once a field has been added, its type cannot change**.

To sum up, Elasticsearch is schema-less in that you do not need to define fields in advance, **but it requires that the fields in documents being indexed are compatible with the mapping.** You can add new fields anytime, but once a field is defined, you cannot change its type.

Summary

In this chapter, we looked at the basic concepts of mapping and reviewed the basic definitions—what the metadata fields are, how does mapping control them—and we examined some data types. Then we looked at the relationship between mapping and relevant search results. Finally, we tried to understand correctly the meaning of schema-less by asking the question: Is the claim about "Elasticsearch stands for the schema-free model" always true?

In the next chapter, you'll learn about the analysis module and analyzers. In addition, we will examine the questions—what is the analysis process? What do the underlying Tokenizer, Token, and CharFilters make?—and some other concepts related to this topic.

4
Analysis and Analyzers

In the previous chapter, we looked at the basic concepts and definitions of mapping. We talked about fields of metadata and data types. Then, we discussed the relationship between mapping and relevant search results. Finally, we tried to have a good grasp of understanding what the schema-less is in Elasticsearch.

In this chapter, we will review the process of analysis and analyzers. We will examine the tokenizers and we will look closely at the character and token filters. In addition, we will review how to add analyzers to an Elasticsearch configuration. By the end of this chapter, we would have covered the following topics:

- What is analysis process?
- What is built-in analyzers?
- What are doing tokenizers, character, and token filters?
- What is text normalization?
- How to create custom analyzers?

Introducing analysis

As mentioned in *Chapter 1, Introduction to Efficient Indexing*, a huge scale of data is produced at any moment in today's world of information technologies on various platforms, such as social media and medium and large-sized companies, which provide services in communication, health, security, and any other areas. Moreover, initially, such data is in an unstructured form.

We can see that this point of view on the *big data* takes into account three basic needs/concerns/forms:

- Recording of data by high performance
- Accessing of data by high performance
- Analyzing of data

Big data solutions are mostly related to the aforementioned three basic needs.

Data should be recorded with high performance in order that data can be accessed with fully high performance benefits; however, it is not enough alone. **To get the real meaning of data, data must be analyzed**.

Thanks to data analysis, the well-established search engines like Google and many social media platforms like Facebook/Twitter are using it successfully.

Let's consider Google with the following screenshot.

Would you accept it if Google does not predict that you're looking for **Barcelona** when you search for the phrase **barca** or if does not ask you the **Did you mean** function when you make a spelling mistake?

To be honest, the answer is absolutely not.

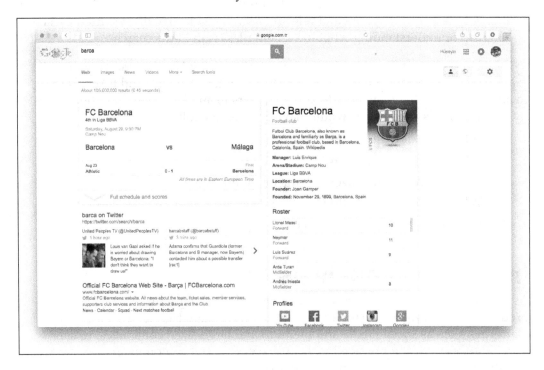

If a search engine does not predict what we're looking for, then we use another search engine that can do it.

We're talking about subtle analysis, and more than that, the exact value of Barca is not the same as the exact value barca. We are talking about the understanding of a search. For example, TR relates to Turkey and a search for Jeffrey Jacob Abrams also relates to J.J. Abrams.

The importance of data analysis occurs at this point because the understanding of the aforementioned analysis can only be achieved by data analysis.

We will discuss the analysis process in Elasticsearch in the next sections.

Process of analysis

We mentioned in *Chapter 1, Introduction to Efficient Indexing* and *Chapter 2, What is an Elasticsearch Index* that all Apache Lucene's data is stored in the *inverted index*. This means that the data is being transformed. The process of transforming data is called analysis. The analysis process relies on two basic pillars: **tokenizing** and **normalizing**.

The first step of the analysis process is to break the text into tokens using tokenizer after processing by the character filters for the inverted index. Then, it normalizes these tokens (that is, terms) to make them easily searchable.

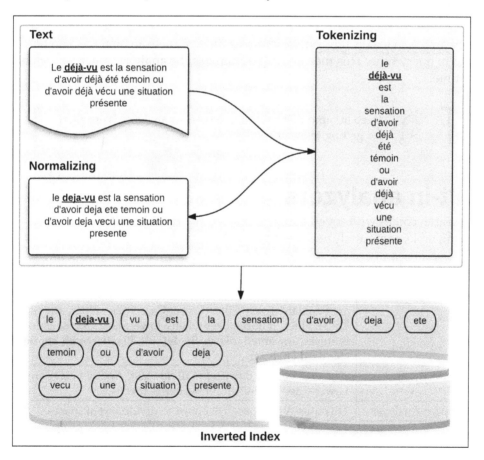

Inverted index processes are performed by analyzers. Generally, an analyzer is composed of a tokenizer and one or more token filters. During the indexing time, when Elasticsearch processes a field that must be indexed, it checks whether an analyzer is defined at several levels or not because an analyzer can be specified at several levels.

The check order is as follows:

1. At field level
2. At type level
3. At index level
4. At node level

 The _analyzer field is used to define document-level analyzer. It is deprecated in 1.5.0 version.

Elasticsearch also makes the control in query time because an analyzer can be defined in query time. This means that you can use the analyzer when you want in query time.

 Keep in mind that choosing the correct analyzer is essential for getting relevant results.

Built-in analyzers

Elasticsearch comes with several analyzers in its standard installation. In the following table, some analyzers are described:

Analyzer	Description
Standard Analyzer	This uses Standard Tokenizer to divide text. Other components are Standard Token Filter, Lower Case Token Filter, and Stop Token Filter. It normalizes tokens, lowercases tokens, and also removes unwanted tokens. **By default, Elasticsearch applies the standard analyzer.**
Simple Analyzer	This uses Letter Tokenizer to divide text. Another component is Lower Case Tokenizer. It lowercases tokens.
Whitespace Analyzer	This uses Whitespace Tokenizer to divide text at spaces.

Analyzer	Description
Stop Analyzer	This uses Letter Tokenizer to divide text. Other components are Lower Case Tokenizer and Stop Token Filter. It removes stop words from token streams.
Pattern Analyzer	This uses a regular expression to divide text. It accepts lowercase and stop words setting.
Language Analyzer	A set of analyzers analyze the text for a specific language. Languages supported are: Arabic, Armenian, Basque, Brazilian, Bulgarian, Catalan, Chinese, Czech, Danish, Dutch, English, finish, French, Galician, German, Greek, Hindi, Hungarian, Indonesian, Irish, Italian, Latvian, Norwegian, Persian, Portuguese, Romanian, Russian, Spanish, Swedish, Turkish, and Thai.

Analyzers fulfill the following three main functions using character filters, tokenizer, and token filters:

- Filtering of characters
- Tokenization
- Filtering of the term

Let's look at the main function of how closely it is realized now.

Building blocks of Analyzer

In the analysis process, a tokenizer is used to break a text into tokens. Before this operation, the text is passed through any character filter. Then, token filters start working.

Character filters

Character filters are used before being passed to tokenizer at the analysis process. Elasticsearch has built-in characters filters. Also, you can create your own character filters to meet your needs.

HTML Strip Char filter

This filter is stripping out HTML markup from an analyzed text. For example, consider the following verse belonging to the Turkish poet and sufi mystic **Yunus Emre**:

```
&#194;&#351;&#305;klar &#246;lmez!
```

As you can see, Turkish and Latin accent characters are used instead of HTML decimal code. The original text is Âşıklar ölmez! (Translation: lovers are immortal!) Let's see how you get a result when this text is analyzed with standard tokenizer:

```
curl -XGET 'localhost:9200/_analyze?tokenizer=standard&pretty' -d
'&#194;&#351;&#305;klar &#246;lmez!'
{
  "tokens" : [ {
    "token" : "194",
    "start_offset" :2,
    "end_offset" :5,
    "type" : "<NUM>",
    "position" : 1
  }, {
    "token" : "351",
    "start_offset" :8,
    "end_offset" :11,
    "type" : "<NUM>",
    "position" : 2
  }, {
    "token" : "305",
    "start_offset" :14,
    "end_offset" :17,
    "type" : "<NUM>",
    "position" : 3
  }, {
    "token" : "klar",
    "start_offset" :18,
    "end_offset" :22,
    "type" : "<ALPHANUM>",
    "position" : 4
  }, {
    "token" : "246",
    "start_offset" :25,
    "end_offset" :28,
    "type" : "<NUM>",
    "position" : 5
  }, {
    "token" : "lmez",
    "start_offset" :29,
    "end_offset" :33,
    "type" : "<ALPHANUM>",
    "position" : 6
  } ]
}
```

As you can see, these results are not useful or user-friendly. Remember, if text is being analyzed in this way, documents containing the word Âşıklar are not returned to us when we search the word Âşıklar. In this case, we need a filter to convert the HTML code of the characters. HTML Strip Char Filter performs this job, as shown:

```
curl -XGET 'localhost:9200/_analyze?tokenizer=standard&char_
filters=html_strip&pretty' -d '&#194;&#351;&#305;klar &#246;lmez!'
{
  "tokens" : [ {
    "token" : "Âşıklar",
    "start_offset" :0,
    "end_offset" :22,
    "type" : "<ALPHANUM>",
    "position" : 1
  }, {
    "token" : "ölmez",
    "start_offset" :23,
    "end_offset" :33,
    "type" : "<ALPHANUM>",
    "position" : 2
  } ]
}
```

Pattern Replace Char filter

This char filter allows using a regex to manipulate the characters. The usage of the filter will be exemplified in the *Creating a Custom Analyzer* section.

Tokenizer

Token is one of the basic concepts in the lexical analysis of computer science, which means that a sequence of characters (that is, string) can turn into a sequence of tokens. For example, the string `hello world` becomes [`hello`, `world`]. Elasticsearch has several tokenizers that are used to divide a string down into a stream of terms or tokens. A simple tokenizer may split the string up into terms wherever it encounters word boundaries, whitespace, or punctuation.

Elasticsearch has built-in tokenizers. You can combine them with character filters to create custom analyzers. In the following table, some tokenizers are described:

Tokenizer	Description
Standard Tokenizer	This finds the boundaries between words and then divides text. To do this, it uses the Unicode Text Segmentation algorithm.
Letter Tokenizer	This divides text at non-letters and converts them to lower case that performs the function of Letter Tokenizer and the Lower Case Token Filter together.
Whitespace Tokenizer	This divides text at spaces.
Pattern Tokenizer	This divides text at via a regular expression.
UAX Email URL Tokenizer	This tokenizes e-mails and URLs as single tokens. It works like the standard tokenizer.
Path Hierarchy Tokenizer	This divides text at delimiters (defaults character delimiter to '/').

 If you want more information about the Unicode Standard Annex #29, refer to http://unicode.org/reports/tr29/.

Token filters

Token filters accept a stream of modified tokens from tokenizers. Elasticsearch has built-in token filters. In the following table, some token filters are described:

Token Filter	Description
ASCII Folding Token Filter	This converts alphabetic, numeric, and symbolic unicode characters that are not in the first 127 ASCII characters.
Length Token Filter	This removes words that are longer or shorter than specified.
Lowercase Token Filter	This normalizes token text to lower case.
Uppercase Token Filter	This normalizes token text to upper case.
Stop Token Filter	This removes stop words (They are specified words - for example the, is, are, and so on.) from token streams.
Reverse Token Filter	This simply reverses each token.
Trim Token Filter	This trims the whitespace surrounding a token.
Normalization Token Filters	These normalize special characters of a certain language (for example, Arabic, German, Persian).

What's text normalization?

Text normalization is the process of transforming text into a common form. That is necessary in order to remove insignificant differences among identical words.

Let's look at *déjà-vu* word to handle.

The word *deja-vu* is not equal to déjà-vu for string comparison. Even *Déjà-vu* is not equal to *déjà-vu*. Similarly, Michè'le is not equal to Michèle. All these words (that is, tokens) are not equal because the comparison is made at the **byte-level** by Elasticsearch. This means, for two tokens to be considered the same, they need to consist of exactly the same bytes when these tokens are compared.

However, these words have similar meanings. In other words, the same thing is being sought when a user is searching for the word *déjà-vu* and another user, *deja-vu* or *deja vu*. It should also be noted that the Unicode standard allows you to create equivalent text in multiple ways.

For example, take letters é (*Latin Capital letter e with grave*) and é (*Latin Capital letter e with acute*). In this case, you may have the same letters encoded in different ways on your data source. Such reasons are necessary for improving relevant search results. **This is the job of token filters** and this process makes tokens more easily searchable.

There are four normalization forms that exist, namely:

- NFC
- NFD
- NFKC
- NFKD

NFC is canonical composition and **NFKC** is compatibility composition. These forms represent characters in the fewest bytes possible. The original word remains unchanged in these forms.

NFD is canonical decomposition and **NFKD** is compatibility decomposition. These decomposed forms represent characters by their constituent parts.

 If you want more information about the unicode normalization forms, refer to http://unicode.org/reports/tr15/

ICU analysis plugin

Elasticsearch has an ICU analysis plugin. You can use this plugin to use mentioned forms in the previous section, and so ensuring that all of your tokens are in the same form. Note that the plugin must be compatible with the version of Elasticsearch in your machine:

```
bin/plugin install elasticsearch/elasticsearch-analysis-icu/2.7.0
```

After installing, the plugin registers itself by default under `icu_normalizer` or `icuNormalizer`. You can see an example of the usage as follows:

```
curl -XPUT /my_index -d '{
  "settings": {
    "analysis": {
      "filter": {
        "nfkc_normalizer": {
          "type": "icu_normalizer",
          "name": "nfkc"
        }
      },
      "analyzer": {
        "my_normalizer": {
          "tokenizer": "icu_tokenizer",
          "filter":  [ "nfkc_normalizer" ]
        }
      }
    }
  }
}'
```

The preceding configuration let's normalize all tokens into the NFKC normalization form.

 If you want more information about the ICU, refer to `http://site.icu-project.org`. If you want to examine the plugin, refer to `https://github.com/elastic/elasticsearch-analysis-icu`.

ASCII Folding Token filter

The ASCII Folding token filter converts alphabetic, numeric, and symbolic unicode characters. It determines their corresponding ASCII characters, if a character is not in the first 127 ASCII characters and, of course, if one exists.

To see how it works, run the following command:

```
curl -XGET '1
ocalhost:9200/_analyze?tokenizer=standard&filters=asciifolding&pretty'
-d "Le déjà-vu est la sensation d'avoir déjà ététémoinoud'avoir déjà
vécuune situation présente"
{
  "tokens" : [ {
    "token" : "Le",
    "start_offset" :0,
    "end_offset" :2,
    "type" : "<ALPHANUM>",
    "position" : 1
  }, {
    "token" : "deja",
    "start_offset" :3,
    "end_offset" :7,
    "type" : "<ALPHANUM>",
    "position" : 2
  }, {
    "token" : "vu",
    "start_offset" :8,
    "end_offset" :10,
    "type" : "<ALPHANUM>",
    "position" : 3
  }, {
    "token" : "est",
    "start_offset" :11,
    "end_offset" :14,
    "type" : "<ALPHANUM>",
    "position" : 4
  }, {
    "token" : "la",
    "start_offset" :15,
    "end_offset" :17,
    "type" : "<ALPHANUM>",
    "position" : 5
  }, {
    "token" : "sensation",
    "start_offset" :18,
    "end_offset" :27,
    "type" : "<ALPHANUM>",
    "position" : 6
  }, {
    "token" : "d'avoir",
```

```
      "start_offset" :28,
      "end_offset" :35,
      "type" : "<ALPHANUM>",
      "position" : 7
    }, {
      "token" : "deja",
      "start_offset" :36,
      "end_offset" :40,
      "type" : "<ALPHANUM>",
      "position" : 8
    }, {
      "token" : "ete",
      "start_offset" :41,
      "end_offset" :44,
      "type" : "<ALPHANUM>",
      "position" : 9
    }, {
      "token" : "temoin",
      "start_offset" :45,
      "end_offset" :51,
      "type" : "<ALPHANUM>",
      "position" : 10
    }, {
      "token" : "ou",
      "start_offset" :52,
      "end_offset" :54,
      "type" : "<ALPHANUM>",
      "position" : 11
    }, {
      "token" : "d'avoir",
      "start_offset" :55,
      "end_offset" :62,
      "type" : "<ALPHANUM>",
      "position" : 12
    }, {
      "token" : "deja",
      "start_offset" :63,
      "end_offset" :67,
      "type" : "<ALPHANUM>",
      "position" : 13
    }, {
      "token" : "vecu",
      "start_offset" :68,
      "end_offset" :72,
```

```
        "type" : "<ALPHANUM>",
        "position" : 14
      }, {
        "token" : "une",
        "start_offset" :73,
        "end_offset" :76,
        "type" : "<ALPHANUM>",
        "position" : 15
      }, {
        "token" : "situation",
        "start_offset" :77,
        "end_offset" :86,
        "type" : "<ALPHANUM>",
        "position" : 16
      }, {
        "token" : "presente",
        "start_offset" :87,
        "end_offset" :95,
        "type" : "<ALPHANUM>",
        "position" : 17
      } ]
  }
```

As you see, even though a user may enter déjà, the filter converts it to deja;
likewise, été is being converted to ete. The ASCII Folding token filter doesn't
require any configuration, but, if desired, you can include directly the one in a
custom analyzer as follows:

```
curl -XPUT localhost:9200/my_index -d '{
   "settings": {
     "analysis": {
       "analyzer": {
         "folding": {
           "tokenizer": "standard",
           "filter":  [ "lowercase", "asciifolding" ]
         }
       }
     }
   }
}'
```

An Analyzer Pipeline

If we have a good grasp of the analysis process described so far, a pipeline of an analyzer should be as shown in the following picture:

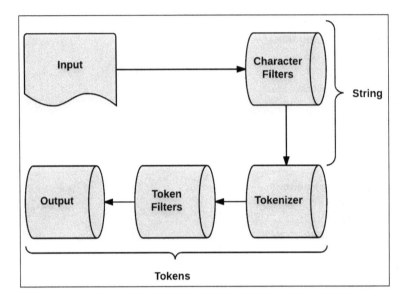

Text to be analyzed is primarily processed by the character filters. Then, a filter divides the text by tokenizers and tokens are obtained. In the final step, the token filters modify tokens.

Specifying the analyzer for a field in the mapping

You can define an analyzer both in the `index_analyzer` and the `search_analyzer` member over a field in the mapping process. Also, Elasticsearch allows you to use different analyzers in separate fields.

The following command shows us the mapping for the fields that an analyzer defined:

```
curl -XPUT localhost:9200/blog -d '{
  "mappings": {
    "article": {
      "properties": {
        "title": {
          "type": "string", "index_analyzer": "simple"
        },
```

```
            "content": {
                "type": "string", "index_analyzer": "whitespace", "search_
    analyzer": "standard"
                }
            }
        }
    }
}'
{"acknowledged":true}
```

We defined a simple analyzer to the `title` field, and `whitespace` analyzer to the `content` field by the preceding configuration. Also, the `search analyzer` refers to the standard analyzer in the content field.

Now, we will add a document to the blog index as follows:

```
curl -XPOST localhost:9200/blog/article -d '{
    "title": "My boss's job was eliminated'",
    "content": "Hi guys. My boss's job at the office was eliminated due
to budget cuts.'"
}'
{"_index":"blog","_type":"article","_id":"AU-bQRaEOIfz36vMy16h","_
version":1,"created":true}

Now we will search boss's word in the title field:

curl -XGET localhost:9200/blog/_search?pretty -d '{
  "query": {
    "match": {
      "title": "boss's"
    }
  }
}'
{
    "took": 2,
    "timed_out": false,
    "_shards": {
        "total": 5,
        "successful": 5,
        "failed": 0
    },
    "hits": {
        "total": 0,
        "max_score": null,
        "hits": []
    }
}
```

Oops, we have a problem.

Actually, we have a document that contains the `boss's` phrase in the `title` field, but the document is not returned by the query. Why did this happen?

To answer this question, let's see how the `boss's` phrase is analyzed in the `title` field using the Analyze API:

```
curl -XGET "localhost:9200/blog/_analyze?field=title&text=boss's&pret
ty"
{
  "tokens" : [ {
    "token" : "boss",
    "start_offset" :0,
    "end_offset" :5,
    "type" : "word",
    "position" : 1
  }, {
    "token" : "s",
    "start_offset" :10,
    "end_offset" :11,
    "type" : "word",
    "position" : 2
  } ]
}
```

As you can see, simple analyzer broke the apostrophe. Now, let's search the phrase `guys` in the `content` field for getting same document:

```
curl -XGET localhost:9200/blog/_search -d '{
 "query": {
   "match": {
     "content": "guys"
   }
 }
}'
{
    "took": 4,
    "timed_out": false,
    "_shards": {
       "total": 5,
       "successful": 5,
       "failed": 0
    },
    "hits": {
```

```
        "total": 0,
        "max_score": null,
        "hits": []
    }
}
```

We have a document that contains the `guys` phrase in the `content` field but the document is not returned by the query. Let's see how the `Hi guys.` sentence is analyzed in the content field using the Analyze API:

```
curl -XGET 'localhost:9200/blog/_analyze?field=content&text=Hi
guys.&pretty'
{
    "tokens": [
        {
            "token": "Hi",
            "start_offset": 0,
            "end_offset": 2,
            "type": "word",
            "position": 1
        },
        {
            "token": "guys.",
            "start_offset": 3,
            "end_offset": 8,
            "type": "word",
            "position": 2
        }
    ]
}
```

As you can see, the whitespace analyzer broke the space and did not remove the punctuation. If we recreate the blog index with the following configuration, in both the preceding query will return documents:

```
curl -XDELETE localhost:9200/blog
{"acknowledged":true}

curl -XPUT localhost:9200/blog -d '{
  "mappings": {
    "article": {
      "properties": {
        "title": {
          "type": "string", "index_analyzer": "simple", "search_
analyzer": "simple"
        },
```

```
        "content": {
          "type": "string"
        }
      }
    }
  }
}'
{"acknowledged":true}
```

In the preceding configuration, we defined a simple analyzer to the `title` field for indexing and search operation. By default, Elasticsearch applies standard analyzer for fields of a document. This is why we did not define an analyzer for the content field. Now the document will return to us when we search a `boss's` phrase.

To summarize this example, when at first we searched the `boss's` word in the `title` field, Elasticsearch did not return any document to us because we used simple analyzer for indexing on the title field, and this analyzer divided the text at non-letters. That means that `boss's` phrase divided the apostrophe by the simple analyzer. However, the title field uses standard analyzer at search time. Remember that we did not define a search analyzer for the title field initially. So, the document was not returned to us because we used two analyzers that have different behaviors for indexing and searching. By eliminating these differences, the document was returned to us.

 Keep in mind that the same analyzer used at index time and at search time is very important for **the terms of the query to match the terms of inverted index**.

Creating a custom analyzer

Although the analyzers that come bundled with Elasticsearch are sufficient for many cases, we may want to use custom analyzers for some special needs by combining character filters, tokenizers, and token filters in a configuration.

For example, if we include the `javaee` phrase or `j2ee` phrase in our article, we want to analyze them as `java enterprise edition`. The following is a sample configuration that allows it:

```
curl -XPUT localhost:9200/my_index -d '{
  "settings" : {
    "analysis" : {
      "char_filter" : {
        "my_pattern":{
          "type":"pattern_replace",
```

```
                "pattern":"j2ee|javaee(.*)",
                "replacement":"java enterprise edition $1"
            }
        },
        "analyzer" : {
            "my_custom_analyzer" : {
                "tokenizer" : "standard",
                "filter":        ["lowercase"],
                "char_filter" : ["my_pattern"]

            }
        }
    }
}'
{"acknowledged":true}
```

The preceding configuration, firstly, defines a character filter. It is a type of `pattern_replace`. We defined a pattern and replacement text for this filter.

Then, we configured our custom analyzer. We gave it a name: `my_custom_analyzer`. The analyzer has standard tokenizer and lowercase token filter, and the character filter is a type of `pattern_replace` that we just created.

This custom analyzer, firstly, uses the character filter to manipulate the characters. Then, it divides text at the word boundaries and finally, normalizes token text to lower case.

Summary

In this chapter, we looked at the analysis process and we reviewed the building blocks of analyzer. After this, we comprehended what the character filters, tokenizers, and token filters are, and how to specify different analyzers in separate fields. Finally, we saw how to create a custom analyzer. In the next chapter, you'll discover the anatomy of an Elasticsearch cluster, what a shard is, what a replica shard is, what a function replica shard performs, and so on. In addition, we will examine the questions, how do we configure my cluster correctly? and how do we determine the correct number of shard and replicas? We will also look at some relevant cases related to this topic.

5
Anatomy of an Elasticsearch Cluster

In the previous chapter, we looked at the analysis process and analyzers. We talked about character filters, tokenizers, and token filters. Then, we reviewed an analyzer pipeline. Finally, we saw how to create a custom analyzer. In this chapter, we will discover the anatomy of an Elasticsearch cluster. We will try to look closely at the core components of an Elasticsearch cluster. In addition, we will examine the question: how do we configure my cluster correctly? By the end of this chapter, we would have covered the following topics:

- What are basic components of an Elasticsearch cluster
- What are key concepts behind distribution architecture
- What primary and replica shards do
- How to choose the right amount of shards and replicas

Basic concepts

An Elasticsearch cluster is a physical and a logical partition of the nodes that are allocated into it. Initially, you don't need to do any configuration for your cluster. When a node is started, Elasticsearch creates a directory based on the defined cluster name and then the node is allocated to this directory. In the background, Elasticsearch created some shards, and probably replicas as well (unless otherwise noted), when you created an index. The generated shards are also allocated in the same node.

Elasticsearch is built to scale. It will be sufficient to increase the number of nodes when more capacity is needed. In this case, the cluster will reorganize itself to take advantage of the extra hardware and will distribute the load. Elasticsearch provides clustering in a good manner, and this ability is one of the most important advantages.

In the following section, we will look closely at the basic components of an Elasticsearch cluster.

Node

A node is a single instance of the Elasticsearch server and it can host data. This means that shards of indices are allowed to be allocated on the nodes. By default, each node is considered to be a data node, but you can turn the setting off.

 You can make a non-data node by adding `node.data: false` to the `elasticsearch.yml` file.

Non-data nodes

There are two types of non-data nodes: dedicated master nodes and client nodes.

Dedicated master nodes

Dedicated master nodes will have the settings `node.data: false` and `node.master: true`. Such nodes are responsible for managing the cluster. Index and search requests are not sent to these nodes.

Client nodes

Client nodes will have the settings `node.data: false` and `node.master: false`. It can be used to balance the load because all HTTP communication will be performed through these nodes.

Tribe node

Another type of Elasticsearch node is **tribe node**. Normally, a node is associated with a single cluster. But sometimes, all the connected clusters may feel the need to get information. In other words, you may want to access data from multiple clusters. The tribe nodes respond to this need. A tribe node acts as a federated client across multiple clusters. The tribe node works to retrieve the state of all connected clusters and merges them into a global cluster state:

```
tribe:
    appellation1:
        cluster.name: cluster_user
    appellation2:
        cluster.name: cluster_employee
```

When configuring a tribe node, it just needs to list the clusters that should be joined. The appellation1 and appellation2 are arbitrary names representing the connection to each cluster.

Shards

When you create an index, Elasticsearch subdivides your index into multiple Lucene indices that are called shards. The process of this subdividing is called **sharding**. Shards are automatically managed by Elasticsearch and are in themselves a fully functional and independent index. You can define a number of shards. By default, a shard is being refreshed per second. **Elasticsearch thus supports real-time search**. Shards are useful when working with large data because when you have a large index, disk capacity of a single node may not be sufficient or may be too slow to serve search requests. Shards solve such, and similar, problems and allow you to horizontally scale your content volume.

Replicas

By default, Elasticsearch creates five primary shards and a copy of each primary shard when you create an index. These copies are called replicas. So, the replica shard is simply a copy of a primary shard. Replica shards are used to improve the search performance and failover. If a node crashes in a way, Elasticsearch uses one of the available replica shards of the node to avoid any data loss. For this reason, **a replica of a primary shard will not be allocated in the same node with the primary shard.** Hence, choosing the right amount of shards and replicas is very important. Unlike primary shards, replicas can be added and removed at any time. The number of primary shards must be specified before creating an index.

Explaining the architecture of distribution

Initially, we don't have an index and data when we start a single node. In this case, it means we have an empty cluster. When we create an index with the default settings, the cluster will take the following view:

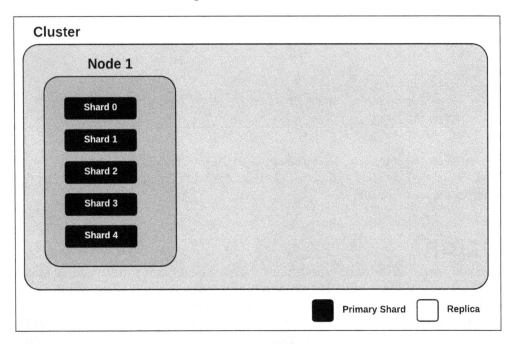

As mentioned earlier, Elasticsearch creates five primary shards and a copy of each primary shard by default. But replicas do not appear in the preceding view. Why?

Let's look for the answer to our question by using the Cat API:

```
curl -XGET 'localhost:9200/_cat/shards'
```

```
my_index 4 p STARTED    0144b 192.168.1.22 Digitek
my_index 4 r UNASSIGNED
my_index 0 p STARTED    0144b 192.168.1.22 Digitek
my_index 0 r UNASSIGNED
my_index 3 p STARTED    0144b 192.168.1.22 Digitek
my_index 3 r UNASSIGNED
my_index 1 p STARTED    0144b 192.168.1.22 Digitek
my_index 1 r UNASSIGNED
my_index 2 p STARTED    0144b 192.168.1.22 Digitek
my_index 2 r UNASSIGNED
```

As you can see, there are five shards in our cluster, their states are STARTED, and there are other five shards, yet their states are UNASSIGNED. These unassigned shards are the replicas. Currently, if we use the cluster health API, we will get the following output:

```
curl -XGET 'localhost:9200/_cat/health?pretty'
```

```
1448644024 19:07:04 elasticsearch yellow 1 1 6 6 0 0 6 0
```

As you can see, the cluster status is yellow. A cluster status can be green, yellow, or red. If a primary shard is not allocated in the cluster, the cluster status will be red. The yellow status means that the primary shard is allocated but replicas are not. Finally, the green status means that all shards are allocated. When we start a new node, the cluster will be formed again, like the following view:

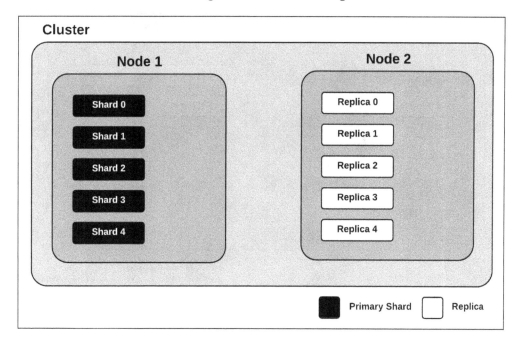

After using the Cat API again, we should now see some differences in the output:

```
curl -XGET 'localhost:9200/_cat/shards'
my_index 2 p STARTED 0144b 192.168.1.22 Digitek
my_index 2 r STARTED 0108b 192.168.1.22 Red Shift
my_index 0 p STARTED 0144b 192.168.1.22 Digitek
my_index 0 r STARTED 0108b 192.168.1.22 Red Shift
my_index 3 p STARTED 0144b 192.168.1.22 Digitek
```

```
my_index 3 r STARTED 0108b 192.168.1.22 Red Shift
my_index 1 p STARTED 0144b 192.168.1.22 Digitek
my_index 1 r STARTED 0108b 192.168.1.22 Red Shift
my_index 4 p STARTED 0144b 192.168.1.22 Digitek
my_index 4 r STARTED 0108b 192.168.1.22 Red Shift
```

Let's use the cluster health API again:

```
curl -XGET 'localhost:9200/_cat/health?pretty'
1448645637 19:33:57 elasticsearch green 2 2 12 6 0 0 0 0
```

As you can see, the cluster status was green because the replicas were allocated to the second node. Now, we add another node to our cluster, and we should see the transformed cluster like the following picture:

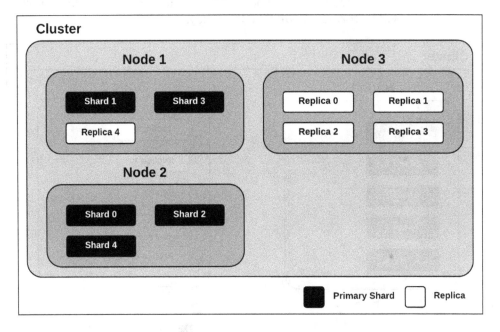

As you have seen, primary shards and replica shards are distributed to the nodes of our cluster. Elasticsearch handles this behavior very wisely. In this way, Elasticsearch can prevent the loss of data when a node is crashed for any reason. Remember that a replica of a primary shard will not be allocated in the same node with the primary shard.

Correctly configuring the cluster

While understanding the distribution of shards is essential, understanding the distribution of documents is also critical. Elasticsearch works to evenly spread the documents at shards. This is an appropriate behavior. Having a shard with the majority of the data cannot be wise.

Let's start two Elasticsearch nodes and create an index by running the following command:

```
curl -XPUT localhost:9200/my_index -d '{
  settings: {
    number_of_shards: 2,
    number_of_replicas: 0
  }
}'
{"acknowledged":true}
```

We've created an index without replicas that are built of two shards. Now we add a document to index:

```
curl -XPOST localhost:9200/my_index/document -d '{
  "title": "The first document"
}'
{"_index":"my_index","_type":"document","_id":"AU_
iaqgDlNVjy8IaI4FM","_version":1,"created":true}
```

```
We will get the current shard level stats of the my_index by using the
following command:
curl -XGET 'localhost:9200/my_index/_stats?level=shards&pretty'
{
...
"shards": {
        "0": [
            {
                "routing": {
                    "state": "STARTED",
                    "primary": true,
                    "node": "8EDJVceZRa2SZeEVTSjtsg",
                    "relocating_node": null
                },
                "docs": {
                    "count": 0,
                    "deleted": 0
                },
                ...
```

```
                    }
                ],
                "1": [
                    {
                        "routing": {
                            "state": "STARTED",
                            "primary": true,
                            "node": "gVKmlQefTqigLiJ7kVRczw",
                            "relocating_node": null
                        },
                        "docs": {
                            "count": 1,
                            "deleted": 0
                        },
                        ...
                    }
                ]
            }
        ...
    }
```

As you can see, there is one document in the second shard. Now we add another document to the `my_index`:

```
curl -XPOST localhost:9200/my_index/document -d '{
  "title": "The second document"
}'
{"_index":"my_index","_type":"document","_id":"AU_
ijSHrlNVjy8IaI4Wu","_version":1,"created":true}
Now we are getting the shard level stats again:
curl -XGET 'localhost:9200/my_index/_stats?level=shards&pretty'
{
...
"shards": {
            "0": [
                {
                    "routing": {
                        "state": "STARTED",
                        "primary": true,
                        "node": "8EDJVceZRa2SZeEVTSjtsg",
                        "relocating_node": null
                    },
                    "docs": {
                        "count": 1,
                        "deleted": 0
```

```
                          },
                          . . .
                      }
                  ],
                  "1": [
                      {
                          "routing": {
                              "state": "STARTED",
                              "primary": true,
                              "node": "gVKmlQefTqigLiJ7kVRczw",
                              "relocating_node": null
                          },
                          "docs": {
                              "count": 1,
                              "deleted": 0
                          },
                          . . .
                      }
                  ]
              }
          . . .
      }
```

As you can see, there is one document in the first and second shards. So, Elasticsearch evenly spread the documents to shards. Now let's kill one node and count the number of documents of the my_index:

```
curl -XGET 'localhost:9200/my_index/_count?pretty'
{
  "count" : 1,
  "_shards" : {
    "total" : 2,
    "successful" : 1,
    "failed" : 0
  }
}
```

Oops, we have a problem. A document is missing. If we control our cluster at this time, we see that the current color of the status is red:

```
curl -XGET 'localhost:9200/_cluster/health?pretty'
{
  "cluster_name" : "elasticsearch",
  "status" : "red",
  "timed_out" : false,
```

```
        "number_of_nodes" : 1,
        "number_of_data_nodes" : 1,
        "active_primary_shards" : 1,
        "active_shards" : 1,
        "relocating_shards" : 0,
        "initializing_shards" : 0,
        "unassigned_shards" : 1,
        "delayed_unassigned_shards" : 0,
        "number_of_pending_tasks" : 0,
        "number_of_in_flight_fetch" : 0
    }
```

When the current color of the status of a cluster is red, it means that all of the primary shards are not active. In this case, losing the data is inevitable. The replica shards solve this problem. If we want to take advantage of the replicas, we should have at least two nodes.

At this point, we might ask: How do we configure the cluster correctly? The question can be answered in two ways. The first way is that the default configuration (which means five shards and one replica) is sufficient to meet basic needs and standard use cases. The second way is that there is no current solution for every situation. There are factors that determine the correct configuration for our cluster. For example, we must know how many nodes we will work, what the size of the data is, and what system resource we have to determine the correct configuration.

First of all, the use of replica is recommended to avoid data loss. To use the replica as said before, there must be at least two nodes. So now, another question arises: How many shards/replicas should we use?

Choosing the right amount of shards and replicas

If you have a limited dataset and the dataset grows by a small amount, you can use only a single primary shard with a replica. If your dataset is not limited and grows by a large amount, the optimal number of shards is dependent on the target number of nodes.

Actually, a single node can be sufficient for many simple use cases, but to reduce the fault tolerance when considering the nature of distributed architecture and to prevent data loss, you can use more than one node. So, we need to find the answer to the first question: How many nodes will work?

Even to answer this question, we need to find out the answers to a few questions. For example: Do we need to use the non-data node? If we don't need to use non-data nodes, considering the Elasticsearch shard allocation policy, we can say that a node requires at least one shard to be the data node - as well as a replica. In that case, we can follow the following formula:

```
Max number of data nodes = number of shards * (number of replicas + 1)
```

Thus, for example, if you have 10 nodes, you can configure our index with the default configuration, which means five shards and one replica. In other words, you can have a maximum of 10 data nodes with the default configuration.

A minimal number of shards is recommended because there is the possible cost of splitting a query into multiple requests to every shard and merging their responses from it. On the other hand, having multiple shards may provide certain advantages. For example, more shards provide faster indexing. More shards refer to more Lucene indexes. Therefore, every operation executed on a smaller index will be faster. To sum up, there are factors that determine the correct configuration and there is no one definite solution for every situation.

Summary

In this chapter, you looked at the basic concepts of an Elasticsearch cluster and saw the core components of it. After this, we discussed how to configure a cluster correctly. Finally, we discussed choosing the right amount of shards and replicas. In the next chapter, you will learn tips to improve indexing performance. We will look at the memory setting and how the optimization of mapping definition improves index performance. In addition, we will examine segment merge policy and will look at some relevant cases related to this topic. And, finally, we will look at the bulk API.

6
Improving Indexing
Performance

In the previous chapter, we looked at the core components of an Elasticsearch cluster. We talked about nodes, shards, and replicas. We tried to explain the architecture of distribution and both shards and documents by Elasticsearch. Then, we looked closely at the functions performed by replica shards. Finally, we discussed how to configure a cluster correctly and how to choose the right amount of shards and replicas. In this chapter, we will look at how we can realize effective indexing. For this purpose, we will examine memory configuration and mapping definition tips. We will look at segments and merging policies. Then, we will examine how to throttle disk I/O operations. By the end of this chapter, we would have covered the following topics:

- How to configure memory for better performance
- The discovery of JVM memory structure
- Types of garbage collector
- Different strategies among garbage collectors
- How to choose the right merge policy
- How to optimize mapping definition to improve index performance
- How to throttle disk I/O operations

Configuration

We have discussed in *Chapter 4, Analysis and Analyzers,* that one of the basic needs in the big data world is the record of data by high performance (if you don't recall, please refer to the Introduction to *Analysis* section in that chapter). This basic need sometimes happens to be the most important priority and you may be willing to sacrifice some other needs for it, for example, search performance and nuanced analysis. In this section, you will find configuration tips for high performance indexing.

Memory configuration

One of the best features of the Java programming language is that memory allocation and deallocation isn't a manual process. Also, the Java programming language has automatic garbage collection, that is, the process to identify and remove unused objects from memory. But still, memory configuration must be done manually to improve performance. The memory configuration is important when speeding up processes. A recommended approach is that when you need to change the JVM settings or arguments for this, use the **ES_JAVA_OPTS** environment variable. At this point, the most important settings are the parameters **-Xmx** and **-Xms**. The first parameter serves to control the maximum allowed memory and the second one controls the initially allocated memory for a process on the JVM heap space. In the following table, some of the commonly used memory parameters are described. Descriptions of the spaces mentioned in this table will be held in the future:

VM Parameter	VM Parameter Description
-Xms	This parameter sets the initial heap size available to the JVM
-Xmx	This parameter sets the maximum heap size available to the JVM
-Xmn	This parameter sets the initial and maximum size of the heap for the young generation as bytes
-XX:PermSize	This parameter sets the space allocated to the permanent generation as bytes. This option was deprecated in JDK 8 and superseded by the -XX:MetaspaceSize option
-XX:MaxPermSize	This parameter sets the maximum permanent generation space size as bytes. This option was deprecated in JDK 8 and superseded by the -XX:MaxMetaspaceSize option
-XX:InitialSurvivorRatio	This parameter sets the initial survivor space ratio used by the through put garbage collector

The JDK 8 HotSpot JVM is now using native memory; it's called Metaspace and has removed permanent generation in the Hotspot JVM.

The ES_HEAP_SIZE environment variable

The **ES_HEAP_SIZE** environment variable can be used to configure -Xmx and -Xms parameters for memory configuration in Elasticsearch that will allocate the same value to both **ES_MIN_MEM** (defaults to 256 m) and **ES_MAX_MEM** (defaults to 1 g) environment variables. The ES_MIN_MEM and the ES_MAX_MEM variables can be set explicitly, but this is not recommended. When we want to pass a value to the JVM, a shell file can be configured for this. An example is seen as follows:

```
# Where does elasticsearch?
export ES_HOME=/usr/local/elasticsearch
export ES_CONF_DIR=$ES_HOME/config
export ES_DATA_DIR=$ES_HOME/data
export CLASSPATH=$ES_HOME/lib/elasticsearch-*.jar:$ES_HOME/lib/*:$ES_
HOME/lib/sigar/*

#This argument to pass to the JVM that allows to set the heap memory
export ES_HEAP_SIZE=1024m

ES_JAVA_OPTS="$ES_JAVA_OPTS -Des.path.data=$ES_DATA_DIR -Des.path.
conf=$ES_CONF_DIR"

export ES_JAVA_OPTS

cd$ES_HOME
exec$ES_HOME/bin/elasticsearch
```

You can retrieve the JVM settings for each node using the Nodes Info API:

```
curl http://localhost:9200/_nodes/jvm?pretty
{
...
"jvm" : {
"pid" : 11628,
"version" : "1.8.0_60-ea",
"vm_name" : "Java HotSpot(TM) 64-Bit Server VM",
"vm_version" : "25.60-b22",
"vm_vendor" : "Oracle Corporation",
"start_time_in_millis" : 1443297108081,
"mem" : {
"heap_init_in_bytes" : 1073741824,
"heap_max_in_bytes" : 1038876672,
"non_heap_init_in_bytes" : 2555904,
"non_heap_max_in_bytes" : 0,
```

```
"direct_max_in_bytes" : 1038876672
        },
...
        }
}
```

Avoiding swapping

Another important issue is swapping, which impacts performance and node stability. The simplest explanation is that swapping is to move the operation of the processes between the disk and memory. The processes are constantly changing place between disk and memory at runtime by the operating system when the memory size is insufficient or the operating system decides that it is better to have some part of memory written into disk. There are time and resources costs of writing the processes into disk for free memory on behalf of higher priority tasks (this is called swap out) and moving back (this is called swap in) when there is enough memory. This can produce bad consequences for performance and for node stability. Therefore, it is recommended to be avoided. Take a look at the following figure:

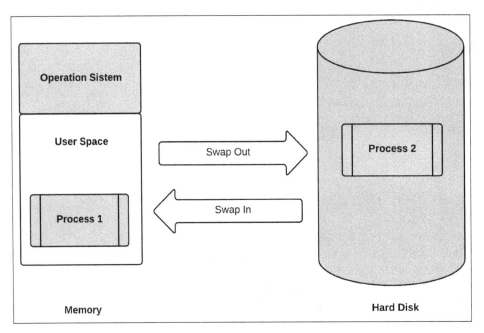

To avoid bad consequences of the swap operations, the `mlockall` property can be enabled.

Mlockall property

The **mlockall** property allows Elasticsearch to lock the heap memory when it sets to `true` in the `elasticsearch.yml` file. The `mlockall` property can be used on Unix systems or VirtualLock on Windows:

```
bootstrap.mlockall: true
```

 If you want more information about the VirtualLock, refer to `https://msdn.microsoft.com/en-us/library/windows/desktop/aa366895%28v=vs.85%29.aspx`.

After giving a `true` value to this property, you can check what was applied successfully using this setting by executing the following command:

```
curl http://localhost:9200/_nodes/process?pretty
{
  "cluster_name" : "elasticsearch",
  "nodes" : {
    ...
      "process" : {
        "refresh_interval_in_millis" : 1000,
        "id" : 5124,
        "max_file_descriptors" : -1,
        "mlockall" : true
      }
    }
  }
}
```

Importantly, while setting the `bootstrap.mlockall` property to `true`, you must be sure that your server has enough free physical memory to start Elasticsearch and leaves enough memory for the operating system. Also, when using this feature, it's recommended to set the ES_MIN_MEM and ES_MAX_MEM variables to the same value because you need to ensure that the JVM resizes the heap with these values.

 Remember, setting the ES_MIN_MEM and ES_MAX_MEM variables explicitly is not recommended. Use the ES_HEAP_SIZE variable instead.

If you see that `mlockall` is `false`, this means that your memory locking is not working. There may be several reasons for this in Unix systems. For example, the user running Elasticsearch doesn't have permission to lock memory, you may need modify some files (like `limits.conf`), the temporary directory is mounted with the noexec option, or if you're using Mac OS X, which only allows their kernel drivers for this, and so on.

Garbage collector

When talking about memory configuration, we need to talk about the garbage collector. In this, first of all, we need to understand the **JVM memory structure** because it is very important if we want to understand the working of **Java garbage collection**.

The structure of JVM memory

JVM memory is divided into separate parts. There are five parts grouped under two main groups called **Young Generation** and **Old Generation**.

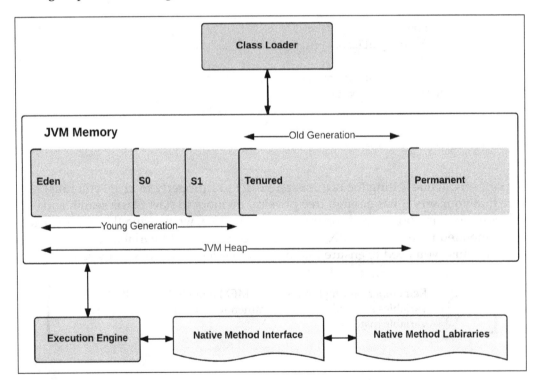

The JVM memory is divided into the following parts:

- **Eden Space**: A part of the heap memory is initially allocated for most of the object types.

- **Survivor Space**: This is a part of the heap memory that has survived the garbage collection of the eden space. The survivor space is divided into survivor space 0 and survivor space 1.

- **Tenured Generation**: This is a part of the heap memory that holds objects that have existed for some time in the survivor space.

- **Permanent Generation**: This is a part of the non-heap memory that holds all the data for the virtual machine itself.

- **Code Cache**: This is a part of the non-heap memory that is present in the HotSpot JVM, which is used for the compilation and storage of native code.

The eden space and the survivor space are called the young generation. In other words, the young generation is divided into three parts: the eden space and two survivor spaces. When a new object is created, it is placed in the eden space. Most of the newly created objects are located here. When the eden space is filled, the young generation garbage collection performed is called **minor GC**.

The minor GC also checks the survivor objects (objects that are unused) and moves them to one of the survivor spaces (first to survivor 0 and then, after another minor GC, to survivor 1). Meanwhile, one of the survivor spaces is always empty. The objects that are survived after living for a while in the survivor 1 space are moved to the tenured generation heap space (that is, old generation heap space).

The old generation space is the place where all the objects are long lived and survived after many cycles of GC. These objects in space will be living as long as the application needs them. Garbage collection is usually performed in old generation heap space when the application no longer needs an object in this space or if there is no free space in old generation heap space. This is called **major GC** and usually takes longer time. After this operation, the garbage collector will make space for new objects.

What is the problem?

When the garbage collector runs, all application threads are frozen until it completes. In the young generation, heap space are located short-lived (relatively new) objects. Therefore, minor GC is very fast and the applications aren't affected too much by this. However, as previously stated, major GC takes longer time because the old generation space is the place where all the objects are long lived, and major GC checks all the live objects in this space.

In this case, your application will be unresponsive during the major GC duration. Hence, it should be minimized. If we have a responsive application that needs to manage many concurrent requests (like an Elasticsearch Server) and major GC is happening frequently, you will notice timeout errors. According to your needs, by monitoring the garbage collector to avoid this from happening, you need to adjust.

Monitoring garbage collection

We can use the Java command line (like `jstat`) or UI tools (like `jconsole`) for monitoring the garbage collection activities of an application. We'll talk about VisualVM with the Visual GC plugin. VisualVM is a user-friendly tool for seeing memory and GC operations.

> If you want more information on how to use the `jstat` command, refer to `http://docs.oracle.com/javase/7/docs/technotes/tools/share/jstat.html`
>
> If you want more information about the JConsole, refer to `https://docs.oracle.com/javase/8/docs/technotes/guides/management/jconsole.html`

VisualVM

First, you don't need to download the VisualVM because it's also part of JDK. You just need to use `jvisualvm` command in the terminal to launch the VisualVM application:

```
$ jvisualvm
```

Once launched, you need to install Visual GC plugin for garbage collector monitoring. For this, you can choose **Tools | Plugings option** in VisualVM main menu and switch to the **Available Plugins** tab; select the **Visual GC plugin**, and click on the **Install** button, as shown in the following image:

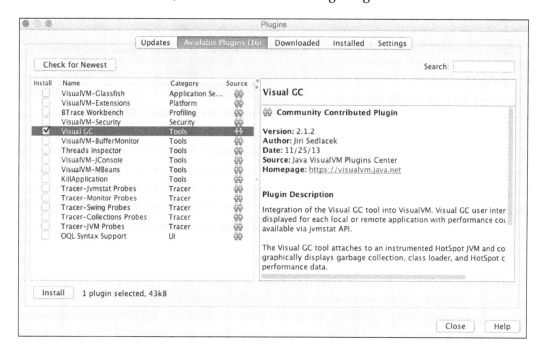

After installing the plugin, the **Visual GC** tab will be added to the VisualVM application. Visual GC attaches to an application and collects and graphically displays garbage collection, class loader, and HotSpot compiler performance data, as shown in the following image:

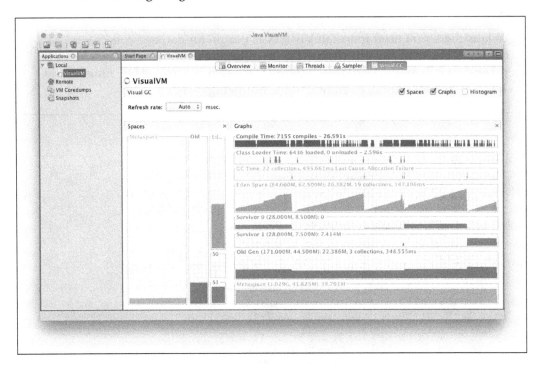

 Monitoring garbage collection is challenging work and usually requires some effort from the system administrator.

 If you want more information about the VisualVM and Visual GC plugin, refer to `https://visualvm.java.net/` as well as `http://www.oracle.com/technetwork/java/visualgc-136680.html`.

Different strategies among garbage collectors

Before coming to the proposals in regard to tuning the garbage collection, we need to talk about the basic process of deallocating memory by the garbage collector and types of garbage collectors. Because each type uses a different strategy, the duration taken by a garbage collector depends on the type of garbage collector, and the process of deallocating memory should be well understood for you to make the right decision in the type selection.

Process of deallocating memory

The process of deallocating consists of the following three steps:

- **Marking**: This is the first step in the process. That is where garbage collector identifies which objects are in use and which are not. In this phase, all objects are scanned to make this determination. Of course, this can be a very time-consuming process.

- **Normal Deletion**: In the second step, garbage collector removes unreferenced objects leaving referenced objects and pointers to free space. The free space can be allocated to other objects.

- **Deletion with Compacting**: After deleting unused objects to improve performance, all the referenced objects can be moved to be together. This makes new memory allocation much easier and faster.

Types of garbage collector

Regarding the types, Java has the following four types of garbage collection types:

- Serial garbage collector
- Parallel garbage collector
- CMS garbage collector
- G1 garbage collector

An administrator or a programmer can choose the type of garbage collector to be used by the JVM. For this, you just need to use a JVM switch. That enables the chosen garbage collection strategy. Let's look at each of them.

Serial garbage collector

Serial garbage collector uses the simple approach. This works by holding all the application threads designed for single-threaded environments. It does the garbage collection for young and old generations. While it runs, all the application threads are frozen. It is best suited for simple standalone applications, as well as simple command-line programs. Use the `-XX:+UseSerialGC` JVM argument to turn it on.

Parallel garbage collector

Parallel garbage collector is the default garbage collector of the JVM. It is also called as Throughput Collector. It's the same as the serial garbage collector, except it uses multiple threads for old generation garbage collection. You can control the number of threads using the `-XX:ParallelGCThreads` JVM option. It works by freezing all the application threads while performing garbage collection like serial garbage collector. Use the `-XX:+UseParallelGC` JVM argument to turn it on.

Concurrent Mark Sweep garbage collector

CMS garbage collector uses multiple threads to scan the heap memory. You can control the number of threads using the `-XX:ParallelCMSThreads` JVM option. It does the garbage collection for old and young generations. The CMS garbage collector holds all the application threads twice during a concurrent collection cycle. The first marks the referenced objects in the old generation space as live. It's referred to as the initial mark pause. The second accounts references that have been changed during the concurrent mark phase in the end of the concurrent tracing phase. It's referred to as the remark pause. The CMS garbage collector tries to minimize the pauses due to garbage collection in this way. It's suitable for responsive applications where we can't afford longer pause times. Compared with parallel garbage collector, CMS consumes more CPU usage, in that the parallel garbage collector ensures better application throughput. Use the `-XX:+UseConcMarkSweepGC` JVM argument to turn it on.

G1 garbage collector

G1 garbage collector is a server-style garbage collector targeted for multi-processor machines. It's used for large heap memory areas. This collector separates the heap memory space into multiple equal-sized heap regions and does collection within them in parallel. It does not work like other collectors, so it does not have young and old generation concepts. The G1 garbage collector prioritizes the region with less live data. Use the `-XX:+UseG1GC` JVM argument to turn it on.

Tuning the garbage collection

If you see the `OutOfMemoryError` exception when monitoring JVM or reviewing in logs, it is a sign that something is wrong with the memory. In this case, either we should consider that we do not have enough memory or we have some memory leak and we do not fully benefit from the available hardware capacity. Before increasing hardware costs, there are things that can be done.

For example, we get an `OutOfMemory` exception. Increasing the PermGen memory space with **-XX:PermGen** and **-XX:MaxPermGen** JVM options could be a solution. Another option is to sweep PermGen and remove classes that are no longer used. The **-XX:+CMSClassUnloadingEnabled** JVM options can be used for this purpose. **Full GC** cleans the entire heap, as well as both young and old spaces. If full GC operations are happening frequently, then you should try increase old generation memory space.

Keep in mind two things. First, this advice may not always work because there is no one definite solution for every situation. You would need to try different options for many cases. Second, tuning the garbage collection should be an option only when you see an application timeout by GC timings.

File descriptors

A file descriptor is an abstract indicator used to access a file on Unix and its derivative operating systems or other I/O resource. It is non-negative integer variable and mostly called FD. Even devices (keyboard, display, and so on) are handled as a file in the other modern operating systems, like on Unix systems. Elasticsearch (actually Lucene) uses a very large number of files. Also, it uses a large number of sockets for communication between nodes, and HTTP clients. Most of the operating systems limit the number of file descriptors and the number of file descriptors allowed per process is inadequate for Elasticsearch. For all of these reasons, you should increase your maximum file descriptor count for the user running Elasticsearch to at least 32k or 64k. To increase the maximum number of file descriptors depends on your operating system; as such, there are different instructions for different Linux distributions.

Increasing FD limit on Unix systems

Although there are different instructions available for different distributions, it is possible to suggest a generally accepted method:

```
sysctl -w vm.max_map_count=1000000
```

You can temporarily set the number of file descriptors with the preceding command on Linux systems. The setting (that is, `vm.max_map_count`) should be changed in your `etc/sysctl.conf` file when you want to set it as the permanent configuration. After changing the settings, you should check to make sure that it worked by executing the following command:

```
curl 'localhost:9200/_nodes/process?pretty'
{
  "cluster_name" : "elasticsearch",
  "nodes" : {
    "CnULkSEWR2i41LLFYcK8Xg" : {

      ...

      ,
      "process" : {
        "refresh_interval_in_millis" : 1000,
        "id" : 7550,
        "max_file_descriptors" : 1000000,
        "mlockall" : false
      }
    }
  }
}
```

There are also different instructions for Mac OS X versions, but the `launchctl` command can be used for increasing the FD limit:

```
sudo launchctl limit maxfiles 10000001000000
```

 After temporarily changing the max file limits with the preceding command, if you see the `10240` value in the `max_file_descriptors` field when you run the `curl 'localhost:9200/_nodes/process?pretty'` command, you have directed the VM to refrain from setting the file descriptor limit to the default `maximum`. In this case, you can pass `-XX:-MaxFDLimit` to stop the Java VM from restricting the number of open files to `10,240`. For more information about this, please the page to which the MaxFDLimit substance is referred: `https://developer.apple.com/library/mac/documentation/Java/Reference/Java_VMOptionsRef/Articles/JavaVirtualMachineOptions.html`.

The setting (that is, `limit maxfiles`) should be changed to different files for different Mac OS X versions when you want to set the permanent configuration. For older Mac OS X versions, you may add the following line to `/etc/launchd.conf`:

```
limit maxfiles 10000001000000#or you want a different value
```

You must update the `kern.maxfiles` and `kern.maxfilesperproc` parameters in the `/etc/sysctl.conf` file for Mountain Lion or Mavericks:

```
kern.maxfiles=1000000
kern.maxfilesperproc=1000000
```

For Yosemite, you have to create a file at `/Library/LaunchDaemons/limit.maxfiles.plist`, as follows:

```xml
<?xml version="1.0" encoding="UTF-8"?>
<!DOCTYPE plist PUBLIC "-//Apple//DTD PLIST 1.0//EN" "http://www.apple.com/DTDs/PropertyList-1.0.dtd">
<plist version="1.0">
<dict>
<key>Label</key>
<string>limit.maxfiles</string>
<key>ProgramArguments</key>
<array>
<string>launchctl</string>
<string>limit</string>
<string>maxfiles</string>
<string>1000000</string>
<string>1000000</string>
</array>
<key>RunAtLoad</key>
<true/>
<key>ServiceIPC</key>
<false/>
</dict>
</plist>
```

Also, if you see the `-1` value in the `max_file_descriptors` field, this means that Elasticsearch is unable to retrieve that value on your operating system.

 Open maximum file descriptors are not supported on Windows platforms. Elasticsearch will always return −1 on Windows platforms.

Optimization of mapping definition

If your search requirements allow it, there are some tips for optimization in the mapping definition of your index for when you need to improve the indexing performance. In the following section, we will look at those tips.

Norms

Scoring is the process of calculating the score of a document in the scope of a particular query and is an important part of the query process in Lucene. The score indicates how well the document matches the query. In other words, it is a factor that shows how close the document you are looking for. This means, the higher the score, the more relevant the document. There are several factors that are a determinant in calculating the score. One of them is the norms.

Lucene takes field length into account for the default relevance calculation. When a searched term is found in a short field (content length is short), Lucene thinks it is more likely that the content of that field is about the term than if the same term contains in a long field (content length is long). Therefore, Lucene keeps the length of a field for later use at query time, that is called *field-length norm*. It is a number that represents the relative field length and boost setting (that is, *this is a match weight factor*). The norms are useful for *scoring* and important for *full-text search*, but this functionality comes at a cost: It requires quite a lot of memory and consumes approximately 1 byte per string field per document in an index. Hence, if you don't need scoring on a specific field, you should disable norms on that field. You can disable the norms before indexing with explicit mapping on a field as follows:

```
curl -XPUT localhost:9200/talent
{
  "mappings": {
    "talented": {
      "properties": {
        "email": {
          "type": "string",
          "norms": {
            "enabled": false
          }
        }
      }
    }
  }
}
{"acknowledged":true}
```

Or by using the PUT mapping API after indexing, like the following:

```
curl -XPUT localhost:9200/talent/_mapping/talented
{
  "properties": {
    "email": {
      "type": "string",
      "norms": {
        "enabled": false
      }
    }
  }
}
{"acknowledged":true}
```

When the norms are disabled in a field, it means that the field will not take the field-length norm into account.

 Norms will not be removed instantly after disabling. They will be removed while you continue indexing new documents because meanwhile, old segments are merged into new segments. In addition, keep in mind that the norms cannot be re-enabled after disabling.

Feature index_option of string type

Elasticsearch provides some features for string types by default. If you don't need these features, you can improve indexing performance by disabling, and therefore, you can save memory. The `index_option` feature allows you to set the indexing options; positions for analyzed fields. This means that doc numbers, term frequencies, and positions will be indexed. Possible values and their meanings are shown in the following table:

Value	Meaning
doc	doc numbers are indexed
freqs	doc numbers and term frequencies are indexed
positions	doc numbers, term frequencies, and positions are indexed

The term frequency is a weight factor that shows how often the term appears in this document. You can disable term frequencies by executing the following command:

```
curl -XPUT localhost:9200/talent
{
  "mappings": {
    "talented": {
      "properties": {
        "zip_code": {
          "type":           "string",
          "index_options": "docs"
        }
      }
    }
  }
}
```

The preceding mapping will disable term frequencies and also term positions at the `zip_code` field, and only doc numbers can be indexed. Keep in mind that the `zip_code` field with this setting will not count how many times a term appears. Also, phrase and proximity queries will not be unable, in that these queries need term frequencies and term positions features when in use. In addition, `not_analyzed` fields use this setting by default.

Exclude unnecessary fields

We mentioned in *Chapter 3, Basic Concepts of Mapping,* that Elasticsearch includes the text of one or more other fields within the document indexed and concatenates them into one big string at _all field. By default, the _all field is enabled. Therefore, maybe you can exclude some fields in the _all field for improving indexing performance and saving disk space. For example, we have `email` and `emailverification` fields and we expect similar content in these fields. In this case, there is no practical benefit if the _all field includes `emailverification` field because the `email` field has already been included in the _all field and this is sufficient to search for an email on _all field. In such cases, you can exclude such fields. Thus, you can improve the performance of indexing and you can reduce your storage costs, and, at the same time, you can throttle unnecessary I/O operations.

 Please refer to the _all section in *Chapter 3, Basic Concepts of Mapping,* about how to exclude a field in the _all field.

Extension of the automatic index refresh time

When the data persistence step comes into play, the hard disk drives are able to create a risk of bottleneck for I/O operations. Elasticsearch uses the filesystem cache that is sitting between itself and the disk for overcoming the risk of bottleneck, so ensure that a new document can be searched in real time. A new segment is written to the filesystem cache first, and later it is flushed to disk by Elasticsearch. (If you do not have information about the segments, you may want to read the *Segments and merging policies* section before this section.) This lightweight process of writing and opening a new segment is called a refresh in Elasticsearch. By default, all shards (so all indices) are being refreshed per second. **Elasticsearch thus supports real-time search**.

Of course, there is a cost to refresh shards per second, especially when working with large size data. You can configure or turn off automatic refresh time. This can be done in the following two ways:

- For all indices in your cluster, by setting the `index.refresh_interval` parameter in the configuration file
- A per-index basis by index setting update

When you want to set an automatic refresh value for all indices in your cluster, you must make the following adjustment in the `elasticsearch.yml` file:

```
index.refresh_interval: 30s
```

The index refresh time has been setting as 30 seconds for all indices in the cluster in the preceding definition. The `index.refresh_interval` setting defines how often the refresh operation will be executed on our indices. Defaults to `1s`. When you set value to `-1`, it means you just turned the setting off. You can set an automatic refresh value for an index, as follows:

```
curl -XPUT localhost:9200/my_index/_settings
{
  "index": {
    "refresh_interval": "30s"
  }
}
```

Extension of the automatic index refresh time enables faster indexing because of memory saving, thus achieving I/O operations throttling. But, in this case, it should be noted that creating new documents and making changes to the existing documents will not appear in searches during a specified period of time.

Segments and merging policies

A Lucene index is composed of smaller chunks that are called segments. In other words, a segment is a section of an index. Each segment is a fully independent index. A new segment can be created when a new document is added or, in the automatic refresh process, it occurs every second by default in Elasticsearch. Each segment consumes system resources (that is, memory, CPU cycles, and so on) and, besides, every segment is checked at search time. This means that if there are more segments, they will be searched and there will be more memory usage. For these reasons, increasing the number of segments is a problem. Small segments are copied to the bigger segment to solve this problem, and the copied segments are deleted from the disk. This operation is called segment merging. It is executed as asynchronous and automatically processes in the background while you are indexing and searching. Segment merging operation saves system resources as well as disk space because old deleted documents are purged from the filesystem at the merge operation.

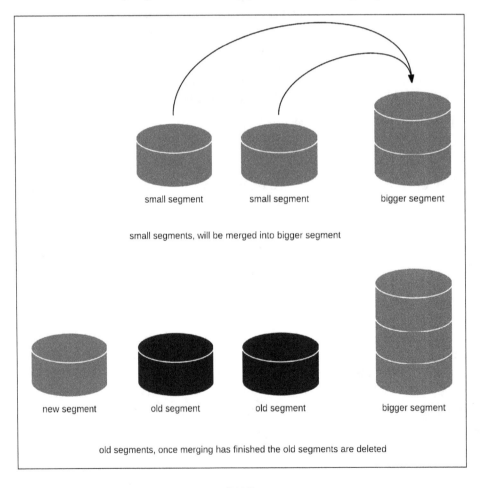

small segment   small segment   bigger segment

small segments, will be merged into bigger segment

new segment   old segment   old segment   bigger segment

old segments, once merging has finished the old segments are deleted

The segments are written once, so they are immutable up to delete markers. In this way, Lucene never has to modify the files of a segment once it has been created. This architecture is preferred to achieve high indexing speed. So, what actually happens when you delete or update a document? Information on a deletion operation is indicated in another file when you delete a document from your index. This means that the deleted documents are only marked as deleted and always stay in the segment. You can get information about segments for a specific index, or several or all indices, and you can see how many deleted documents it has, how much memory use it has, how much disk space use it has, and other details with using *_Indices Segments API*:

```
curl -XGET 'http://localhost:9200/my_index/_segments?pretty'
{
  "_shards" : {
    "total" : 10,
    "successful" : 5,
    "failed" : 0
  },
  "indices" : {
    "my_index" : {
      "shards" : {
        "0" : [ {
          "routing" : {
            "state" : "STARTED",
            "primary" : true,
            "node" : "C6bMfcfQRxS2qEhNktuRqA"
          },
          "num_committed_segments" : 9,
          "num_search_segments" : 9,
          "segments" : {
            "_g7" : {
              "generation" : 583,
              "num_docs" : 1166,
              "deleted_docs" : 23,
              "size_in_bytes" : 3911931,
              "memory_in_bytes" : 1684666,
              "committed" : true,
              "search" : true,
              "version" : "4.10.4",
              "compound" : false
            },

          . . .
```

Even if you delete many documents from your index, until the merge happens, those documents are not deleted from the disk. Similar case is applied for updated documents. In fact, when a document is updated, the old version of the document is marked as deleted in its segment and the actual version of the document is added to the current segment. Good news. In the segment merging time, deleted and old versions of updated documents are not copied over to the bigger segment. After this process, the old segments will be deleted. Deleting old segments reduces the number of segments. This also provides faster search performance. Despite all these advantages, segment merging is an expensive process in terms of I/O (that is, input/output) operations. Therefore, it should be checked.

Choosing the right merge policy

Elasticsearch allows us to choose the merge policy to control which segments of a shard index are being merged. There are three options, which are as follows:

- `tiered`
- `log_byte_size`
- `log_doc`

We will examine each of these three policies. First, let's see how we can define a policy:

```
index.merge.policy.type: tiered
```

With the preceding definition in the elasticsearch.yml configuration file, the merge policy is `tiered`.

Tiered policy

Elasticsearch uses the tiered policy by default. It merges segments of approximately equal size, taking into account the maximum number of segments allowed per tier. During indexing, this policy first computes how many segments are allowed to be present in the index, which is called budget. If the number of segments of the index, then the policy sorts segments by decreasing size, taking into account the deleted documents, and then finds the least-cost merge. This policy has the following settings:

- **index.merge.policy.expunge_deletes_allowed**: This setting specifies the percentage of deleted documents in a segment. When running `expungeDeletes`, Elasticsearch only merges away a segment if its delete percentage is over this threshold. Default is 10.
- **index.merge.policy.floor_segment**: This setting avoids frequent flushing of tiny segments. Segments that are less than the value defined by this setting are rounded up to the specified size of this setting. Default is 2 MB.

- **index.merge.policy.max_merge_at_once**: This setting specifies the maximum number of segments that will be merged at the same time during normal merging. Default is 10.

- **index.merge.policy.max_merge_at_once_explicit:** This setting specifies the maximum number of segments that will be merged at a time during optimize operation or `expungeDeletes`. Default is 30.

- **index.merge.policy.max_merged_segment**: This setting specifies the maximum size of a single segment as approximate that will be produced during normal merging. The estimate of the merged segment size is calculated by summing the size of segments that are compensated for the percentage of deleted documents in those segments. Default is 5 GB.

- **index.merge.policy.segments_per_tier**: This setting specifies the number of segments per tier. It causes the formation of fewer segments and more merging when a low value is defined. This means lower indexing performance. Also, this value needs to be higher than or equal to the `index.merge.policy.max_merge_at_once`; otherwise, you'll force too many merges to occur. Default is 10.

- **index.merge.policy.reclaim_deletes_weight**: This setting specifies how aggressively merges that reclaim deletes are favored. Higher values will lead the more favored merge that will reclaim deletes. Defaults to 2.0.

- **index.compound_format**: This setting is a Boolean or float value that specifies whether the index should be stored in a compound format or not. Default value is `false`. When set to `true`, Lucene will build the index in a single file.

> The compound format functionality is experimental. This means that it may be changed or removed completely in a future release.

When tiered policy is used, and if a merge will produce a segment that is larger than the value specified by the `index.merge.policy.max_merged_segment` setting, the policy will merge fewer segments to keep the segment size under the budget. This can mean that it holds many gigabytes of data for indices that have large shards. This situation may happen when the default value of the `index.merge.policy.max_merged_segment` setting is too low for your case and will slow down your queries because it is created of many segments. You can increase the value of `index.merge.policy.max_merged_segment` setting when needed by monitoring your data with the Indices Segments API or you can use Optimize API that forces a shard to be merged down to the number of segments for that specified number.

Please refer to the *optimize API* section in this chapter for the API description.

log_byte_size policy

This policy is similar to tiered merge policy that merges segments into levels of exponentially increasing byte size, where each level has fewer segments than the value of the merge factor. When extra segments are encountered that are greater than the merge factor, all segments within the level are merged. This policy has the following settings:

- **index.merge.policy.merge_factor**: This setting specifies how often segment indices are merged during indexing. Smaller values cause less RAM usage while indexing and searches are faster on unoptimized indices, but indexing speed is slower. Larger values cause more RAM consumption during indexing, and while searches on unoptimized indices are slower, indexing is faster because less merging is being done. By default, the merge_factor is given the value of 10. Larger values (for example, *greater than the default value*) are recommended for batch index creation and smaller values (for example, *lower than the default value*) are recommended for normal index maintenance.

- **index.merge.policy.min_merge_size**: This setting defines the minimum total size of the segment files in bytes for the lowest level segments. If any segment is lower in size than the number specified by this setting, it will be merged when the merge_factor property allows us to do that. Defaults to 1.6 MB and it effectively avoids having many very small segments. If you set this as too large a value, it will increase the merging cost.

- **index.merge.policy.max_merge_size**: This setting defines the maximum size of the segment based on the total size of the segment files that can be merged with other segments. It defaults to unbounded. This means that there is no limit on the maximum size a segment can be in order to be merged.

- **index.merge.policy.max_merge_docs**: This setting defines the largest segment based on the number of documents that may be merged with other segments. It defaults to unbounded. This means there is there no limit on the maximum number of documents a segment can have.

 Elasticsearch developers say that the log_byte_size policy will be removed in 2.0 in favor of the tiered merge policy. Elasticsearch 2.0.0-rc1 was released when this book was being written.

Log_doc policy

This policy tries to merge segments into levels of exponentially increasing document count as opposed to `log_byte_size` policy where each level has fewer segments than the value of the merge factor. When extra segments are encountered that are greater than the merge factor, all segments within the level are merged. This policy has the following settings:

- **index.merge.policy.merge_factor**: This setting is same as the `index.merge.policy.merge_factor` setting of the `log_byte_size` policy, so please refer to that policy for explanation.

- **index.merge.policy.min_merge_docs**: This setting defines the minimum number of documents for the lowest level segments. Except the default value, it is similar to the `index.merge.policy.min_merge_size` setting of `log_byte_size` policy, so please refer to that policy for explanation. Defaults to 1000.

- **index.merge.policy.max_merge_docs**: This setting is same as the `index.merge.policy.max_merge_docs` setting of `log_byte_size` policy, so please refer to that policy for explanation.

> The log_doc policy has been deprecated since 1.6.0 and Elasticsearch developers say that this policy will be removed in 2.0 in favor of the tiered merge policy. Elasticsearch 2.0.0-rc1 was released when this book was being written.

The optimize API

Elasticsearch provides the optimize API to force segments merging. You can define a number with the `max_num_segments` parameter, and the optimize API on the basis of this definition forces a shard to be merged down to the number of segments. This is usually done to improve search performance:

```
curl -XPOST localhost:9200/my_index/_optimize?max_num_segments=1
```

With the preceding command, Elasticsearch merges each shard in the `my_index` down to a single segment. Keep in mind that even though the optimize API is useful in certain situations, its usage is not recommended since the normal merge process is executed successfully by Elasticsearch.

> This functionality provided by the optimize API comes at a cost-it may consume all of the I/O on your nodes and may cause the cluster to be unresponsive.

Store module

As the name suggests, the store module is related to controlling how index data is stored. All the operations on the hard disk drive are done using the store module. Therefore, when it comes to improving indexing performance, they need to focus on the store module. There are some tips to improve performance for this situation.

Store types

Elasticsearch allows an index to be stored on disk or in memory. By default, it uses filesystem based on storage, and, in this context, it provides some store types that we can use. Elasticsearch will automatically choose the best one for the operating environment. If you would like to use one of these store types, you should set the index.store.type in elasticsearch.yml file:

```
index.store.type: niofs
```

Or it can be set per-index basis at index creation time:

```
curl -XPUT localhost:9200/my_index -d '{
    "settings": {
        "index.store.type": "niofs"
    }
}'
```

Now let's look at these store types one by one.

Simple filesystem store

The **simplefs** type uses a random access file that maps to *Lucene SimpleFSDirectory*. This type is sufficient for very simple applications, but has poor concurrent performance because multiple threads will bottleneck. When you need index persistence, it is usually better to use the new I/O based system store (that is, niofs) instead of the simple FS store.

> If you want more information about the Java RandomAccessFile Class, refer to http://docs.oracle.com/javase/8/docs/api/java/io/RandomAccessFile.html. Also, if you want more information about the Lucene SimpleFSDirectory, refer to https://lucene.apache.org/core/5_3_1/core/org/apache/lucene/store/SimpleFSDirectory.html.

New IO filesystem store

The **niofs** type uses the FileChannel from the `java.nio` package that maps to *Lucene NIOFSDirectory*. It provides a better performance in managing concurrent requests because it allows multiple threads to read from the same file concurrently. The niofs type is not recommended on Windows because a bug exists in the JVM in the SUN Java implementation.

> If you want more information about the bug, refer to `http://bugs.sun.com/bugdatabase/view_bug.do?bug_id=6265734`. Also, if you want more information about the Java FileChannel Class, refer to `http://docs.oracle.com/javase/8/docs/api/java/nio/channels/FileChannel.html`. In addition, if you want more information about the Lucene NIOFSDirectory, refer to `http://lucene.apache.org/core/5_3_1/core/org/apache/lucene/store/NIOFSDirectory.html`.

MMap filesystem store

The **mmapfs** type stores the shard index on the filesystem by mapping a file into memory that maps to *Lucene MMapDirectory*. It uses the `mmap system call` for reading, and random access file for writing. Memory mapping uses a portion of the available virtual memory address space in your process equal to the size of the file being mapped. Therefore, you must make sure that the virtual address space is plentiful. This type is scalable even when it comes to multithread access because it doesn't have any locking and it allows to directly access the I/O cache; thus, fast accessibility to index files.

> If you want more information about the Lucene MMapDirectory, refer to `http://lucene.apache.org/core/5_3_1/core/org/apache/lucene/store/MMapDirectory.html`. Also, if you want more information about the mmap system call, refer to `https://en.wikipedia.org/wiki/Mmap`.

Hybrid filesystem store

The **default** type uses both `MMap` and `Java NIO` access for storage, depending on the file type. Currently only the `term dictionary` and `doc values` files are memory mapped to this type to reduce impact on the operating system. All the other files of the index are opened using *Lucene NIOFSDirectory*.

Throttling I/O operations

As we mentioned in segments and merging policies section, the segments are written once and are immutable up to delete markers. However, they can be read many times. The merge process is asynchronous and is not expected to have a negative effect on the indexing with searching in general. Despite all this, the merging process is expensive in terms of I/O because many read/write operations happen on many files. Usually, searching and indexing happen concurrently on Elasticsearch. In this case, there is a risk of a bottleneck for I/O operations, especially on systems with low I/O.

Fortunately, the store module allows throttling for all writes/merges operations. The throttling can be configured either on a node level or on the index level.

Throttling type

Node level throttling is recommended because all the shards on the same node perform their duty on the same disk I/O operations. In order to configure throttling type on node level, you can use the `indices.store.throttle.type` and `indices.store.throttle.max_bytes_per_sec` settings. The meaning of possible values of the `indices.store.throttle.type` setting is as follows:

- **none**: There is no limit for merging of nodes.
- **merge**: It is I/O will limit the use for merging for nodes. It is the default value.
- **all**: It is I/O will limit the use for all store module based operations.

The `indices.store.throttle.max_bytes_per_sec` setting can be a value such as 5 MB. Its default value is 20 MB with type merge. The node level settings can be changed dynamically using the Cluster Update Settings API, as follows:

```
curl -XPUT localhost:9200/_cluster/settings -d '{
    "persistent" : {
        "indices.store.throttle.type": "all"
    }
}'
{
    "acknowledged": true,
```

```
    "persistent": {
        "indices": {
            "store": {
                "throttle": {
                    "type": "all"
                }
            }
        }
    },
    "transient": {}
}
```

In order to configure throttling type on the index level one, you can use the `index.store.throttle.type` setting. With an additional value that is `node`, it can take the same values as the `indices.store.throttle.type` setting. The node value means use the node level configuration. This is the default value. Also, you can use the `index.store.throttle.max_bytes_per_sec` setting for the index level throttling configuration. The aforementioned settings can be set in the elasticsearch.yml file and can also be updated dynamically using the *Cluster Update Settings API*.

 The node level throttling defaults since Elasticsearch 0.90.1. If you are using an older version, you don't have this option enabled by default.

Bulk API

The bulk API allows to perform many index/delete operations in a single API call. It can greatly increase the indexing speed and should be preferred for optimal performance.

You can use the bulk API as follows:

```
curl -XPUT localhost:9200/_bulk --data-binary @/Users/hakdogan/
Desktop/bulk.json
```

We're providing text file input to curl in the preceding command; therefore, we must use the `--data-binary` flag instead of plain `-d`. After the data flag, the full path of the file beginning should be noted with the @ symbol. The contents of the file are as follows:

```
{ "create" : { "_index" : "my_index", "_type" : "my_type", "_id": 1} }
{ "title":"How to use the Bulk API"}
{ "create" : { "_index" : "my_index", "_type" : "my_type", "_id": 2} }
{ "title":"Sizing bulk requests"}
```

If a document with the same index and type exists already, the request will fail for the `create` action. The following is an example of how to use the `update` and `delete` actions:

```
{ "update" : { "_index" : "my_index", "_type" : "my_type", "_id": 1} }
{ "doc": { "title":"How to use the Bulk API for indexing speed"} }
{ "delete" : { "_index" : "my_index", "_type" : "my_type", "_id": 2} }
```

In the preceding example, we provided index and type names explicitly in the file. If you provide the index or the index/type names in the command line, they will be used by default on bulk items that do not provide them explicitly. Also note that the file format uses literal \n's as delimiters. You should pay attention to it.

 You must be sure that the client does not send HTTP chunks when using the HTTP API because this attempt will slow your work down.

Bulk sizing

Bulk sizing is important, especially when working with large data. It is important to know that there is no correct size of bulk request to perform in a single bulk action. There are some factors at this point, for example, physical size of documents (not document count of an index), cluster configuration, and so on. Ideal size will change for different situations. So, there is no current solution for every situation. Nevertheless, 5–10 MB per bulk can be recommended for the beginning. You can slowly increase it until you do not see performance gains anymore by monitoring your nodes. You can use the `BulkProcessor` class for performing bulk sizing. It has `setBulkSize` method, it takes a parameter of type `ByteSizeValue`. This parameter defines at which size we want to flush the bulk.

Notes

As we mentioned in *Chapter 1, Introduction to Efficient Indexing,* understanding the difference between storable and searchable fields is important for indexing performance and relevant search results. Elasticsearch always stores every document field within the _source field by default. You can change this behavior for some fields that are not really needed to be return. It provides indexing performance and reduces your storage costs.

Also, as we mentioned in *Chapter 5, Anatomy of an Elasticsearch Cluster,* shards and the number of replicas affect the indexing speed. For example, having more shards provides faster indexing. Therefore, every operation executed on a smaller index will be faster.

Summary

In this chapter, we looked at some memory configuration, mapping definition tips, and segments and merging policies. Then, we examined store modules and how to throttle disk I/O operations. Finally, we discussed the bulk API. In the next chapter, we will examine the snapshot and restore modules; this API provides backup and restore operations on your data.

7
Snapshot and Restore

In the previous chapter, we looked at some memory configuration and tips of mapping definition for improving indexing performance. We talked about segments and merging policies. We tried to explain the store module and how to throttle disk I/O operations. Then, we discussed the bulk API. In this chapter, we will look at how can we back up our data and restore. For this purpose, we will examine Elasticsearch snapshot and restore module. By the end of this chapter, we would have covered the following topics:

- How to create a snapshot repository
- How to create a snapshot
- How to restore a snapshot
- How the snapshot process works

Snapshot repository

When working with large amounts of data, backup and restore is an important requirement. Elasticsearch has a snapshot and restore module so that they meet the needs of users for backing up and restoring existing indices. Because Elasticsearch needs to know where to back up data, before backup and restore operations of the indices, a snapshot repository should be registered in Elasticsearch. The following is an example of how to register a snapshot repository:

```
curl -XPUT localhost:9200/_snapshot/my_backup -d '{
    "type": "fs",
    "settings": {
        "location": "/data/backups/my_backup",
        "compress": true,
        "chunk_size": "10m"
    }
}'
```

The preceding command registers a shared filesystem repository named as my_backup. It will use location of /data/backups/my_backup. The _snapshot is a REST endpoint for snapshot operations. Its first parameter is the repository name. Repository name will be specified by this parameter and must be unique. The type parameter defines the information of where snapshot files will be stored. The fs value specifies to use the shared filesystem. The repository settings will vary according to the type of repository. For this reason, now we'll talk about repository types, but, first, let's see how we can delete a repository:

```
curl -XDELETE localhost:9200/_snapshot/my_backup
```

When a repository is deleted, snapshot files of this repository are not deleted because Elasticsearch only removes the reference of location of snapshot files.

Repository types

Elasticsearch initially was supporting only shared filesystem repository, but it currently supports HDFS filesystem and cloud repositories like Amazon S3 and Azure Cloud via officially supported plugins in addition to shared filesystem repository. Now, let's examine those types.

Shared filesystem repository

A shared filesystem repository uses the shared filesystem to store snapshots. It is defined by giving a fs value to the type setting. There are six settings that can be used for the shared filesystem repository. These are as follows:

- location
- compress
- chunk_size
- concurrent_streams
- max_restore_bytes_per_sec
- max_snapshot_bytes_per_sec

The location parameter is mandatory for shared filesystem repository. It defines the path to store files of a snapshot. You must define the same location or one of its parent directories to mount the same shared filesystem for this definition in the elasticsearch.yml file:

```
path.repo: ["/Users/hakdogan/data"]
```

This location has been registered in the `path.repo` setting on all master and data nodes by the preceding definition. Note that this location must be accessible on all nodes. The `compress` setting defines the compression policy of the snapshot files. The default value is true. Files with a large size can be broken down into chunks during snapshotting if desired. The `chunk_size` setting defines the chunk size to be used at during snapshot creation.

You can specify the size as bytes or by using size value notation, that is, `20k`, `10m`, `1g`. The default value is null. There is no correct size of chunk while creating a snapshot. The correct size will vary according to the size of the index files and depending on the system resources you have. Nevertheless, 10m can be recommended. The `concurrent_streams` setting defines number of concurrent read/write stream per repository on each node. Default value is 5. The `max_restore_bytes_per_sec` setting defines throttles per node restore rate. The `max_snapshot_bytes_per_sec` setting defines throttles per node snapshot rate. The default value is 40 MB per second in both settings.

> These two settings are common settings that apply to all repository types.

URL repository

A URL repository is used to read snapshots that were created by the shared filesystem repository. This is an alternative way as read-only to access the data. The following settings are supported:

- `url`
- `concurrent_streams`

The `url` parameter is mandatory for the URL repository. It defines the location of the snapshots to read. You must define the root directory of the shared filesystem repository. The `concurrent_streams` setting defines number of concurrent read/write stream per repository on each node. Default value is 5.

The `http`, `https`, `ftp`, `file`, and `jar` protocols are supported by URL repository. Allowed URLs on the `repositories.url.allowed_urls` setting must be defined when using the URL repositories with `http`, `https`, and `ftp` protocols. This setting supports wildcards (that is, you can use ? symbol instead of a single character and the * symbol instead of multiple characters), as follows:

```
repositories.url.allowed_urls: ["http://www.mydomain.com/root/*",
    "https://*.mydomain.com/*?#*"]
```

Cloud repository

As noted at the beginning of the repository types section, Elasticsearch supports cloud repositories via officially supported plugins. In the following table, these plugins are described:

Plugin	Description	URL
AWS Cloud Plugin	This plugin allows you to use AWS API for the unicast discovery mechanism and add S3 repositories	`https://github.com/elastic/elasticsearch-cloud-aws`
Azure Cloud Plugin	This plugin allowsyou to use Azure API for the unicast discovery mechanism	`https://github.com/elastic/elasticsearch-cloud-azure`

HDFS filesystem repository

Elasticsearch allows you to use the HDFS filesystem as a repository for snapshot and restore with the Hadoop HDFS Snapshot/Restore plugin. There are two requirements, which are as follows:

- Elasticsearch version 2.0 or higher
- HDFS accessible filesystem from the Elasticsearch classpath

> For other and more details, refer to `https://github.com/elastic/elasticsearch-hadoop/tree/master/repository-hdfs`.

Snapshot

A snapshot is a backup of your cluster index(s). Snapshots are stored in a repository that has been registered before. A repository can contain multiple snapshots of the same cluster. A snapshot can be created by executing the following command:

```
curl -XPUT localhost:9200/_snapshot/my_backup/first_snapshot
```

The _snapshot is REST endpoint for snapshot operations. Its second parameter is a unique snapshot name. The preceding command creates a snapshot of all open and started indices in the cluster. If you want to back up a certain index, you must specify the list of indices in the body of the request:

```
curl -XPUT localhost:9200/_snapshot/my_backup/first_snapshot -d '{
  "indices": "my_index",
```

```
    "ignore_unavailable": "true",
    "include_global_state": false,
    "partial": true
}'
```

The `indices` parameter supports `multi-index syntax`; that means you can separate the index names with commas or you can use a wildcard, like `*`. Default value of the `ignore_unavailable` parameter is `true`. It will cause indices that do not exist to be ignored during snapshot creation. If this behavior is not desired, the value of the parameter should be set to `false`. The `include_global_state` setting allows us to store the global state as part of the snapshot. If you want to restore the snapshot into a different cluster, the `include_global_state` parameter should be set to `false`. By default, the snapshot operation will fail when one or more indices don't have all primary shards available. This behavior can be changed by setting the `partial` parameter to `true`.

By default, a snapshot request should return immediately after snapshot initialization. This behavior can be changed by setting the `wait_for_completion` parameter to `true`, as follows:

```
curl-XPUT localhost:9200/_snapshot/my_backup/first_snapshot?wait_for_
completion=true
```

Even when the `wait_for_completion` parameter is set to `false`, the snapshot request may take longer to return in some cases because during snapshot initialization, information on the all previous snapshots is loaded into memory. Therefore, if you have large repositories, the snapshot request to return may take several seconds or even minutes. After you create a snapshot, its information can be obtained using the following command:

```
curl -XGET localhost:9200/_snapshot/my_backup/first_snapshot
{
    "snapshots": [
        {
            "snapshot": "first_snapshot",
            "version_id": 1070199,
            "version": "1.7.3",
            "indices": [
"my_index"
            ],
            "state": "SUCCESS",
            "start_time": "2015-10-24T20:06:27.465Z",
            "start_time_in_millis": 1445717187465,
            "end_time": "2015-10-24T20:06:27.996Z",
            "end_time_in_millis": 1445717187996,
```

```
                "duration_in_millis": 531,
                "failures": [],
                "shards": {
                    "total": 5,
                    "failed": 0,
                    "successful": 5
                }
            }
        ]
    }
}
```

You can obtain information of all snapshots using the _all parameter:

```
curl -XGET localhost:9200/_snapshot/my_backup/_all
```

Also, you can get more and complete status information about currently running snapshots using the following command:

```
curl -XGET localhost:9200/_snapshot/_status
```

The preceding command will return information about all currently running snapshots. You can use the following command if you want to get status information about snapshots belonging to only a particular repository:

```
curl -XGET localhost:9200/_snapshot/my_backup/_status
```

If you want to get detailed status information about a snapshot, you must give the repository and snapshot name as following. In this case, Elasticsearch will return detailed status information for the given snapshot even if it's not currently running:

```
GET /_snapshot/my_backup/first_snapshot/_status
{
    "snapshots": [
        {
            "snapshot": "first_snapshot",
            "repository": "my_backup",
            "state": "SUCCESS",
            "shards_stats": {
                "initializing": 0,
                "started": 0,
                "finalizing": 0,
                "done": 5,
                "failed": 0,
                "total": 5
            },
            "stats": {
                "number_of_files": 65,
```

```
            "processed_files": 65,
            "total_size_in_bytes": 18176267,
            "processed_size_in_bytes": 18176267,
            "start_time_in_millis": 1445873862080,
            "time_in_millis": 413
        },
        "indices": {
            "my_index": {
                "shards_stats": {
                    "initializing": 0,
                    "started": 0,
                    "finalizing": 0,
                    "done": 5,
                    "failed": 0,
                    "total": 5
                },
                "stats": {
                    "number_of_files": 65,
                    "processed_files": 65,
                    "total_size_in_bytes": 18176267,
                    "processed_size_in_bytes": 18176267,
                    "start_time_in_millis": 1445873862080,
                    "time_in_millis": 413
                },
                "shards": {
                    "0": {
                        "stage": "DONE",
                        "stats": {
                            "number_of_files": 13,
                            "processed_files": 13,
                            "total_size_in_bytes": 3910310,
                            "processed_size_in_bytes": 3910310,
                            "start_time_in_millis": 1445873862234,
                            "time_in_millis": 164
                        }
                    },
                    ...
                }
            }
        }
    }
]
}
```

You can get status information about multiple snapshots, as follows:

```
curl-XGET localhost:9200/_snapshot/my_backup/first_snapshot,second_
snapshot/_status
```

And, finally, a snapshot can be deleted using the following command:

```
curl -XDELETE localhost:9200/_snapshot/my_backup/first_snapshot
```

Note that the snapshot delete command can also be used to terminate snapshot process when it is running.

Restore

A snapshot can be restored using the following command:

```
curl -XPOST localhost:9200/_snapshot/my_backup/first_snapshot/_restore
```

The `_restore` is the REST endpoint for restore operations. It restores the snapshot mentioned in the previous parameter. The preceding command will restore all indices of the specified snapshot name. If you want to restore just certain indices, you must be specify the list of indices in the body of the request:

```
curl -XPOST localhost:9200/_snapshot/my_backup/first_snapshot/_restore
-d '{
  "indices": "my_index",
  "ignore_unavailable": "true",
  "include_global_state": false,
  "include_aliases": false,
  "partial": true,
  "rename_pattern": "my_(.+)",
  "rename_replacement": "restored_$1"
}'
```

The `indices` parameter defines the index names that need to be restored. It supports multi-index syntax. For example, when the * character is used, Elasticsearch will restore all indices of the specified snapshot. If you do not want to restore the aliases, the `include_aliases` parameter should be set to `false`.

By default, the restore operation will fail if one or more indices that need to be restored don't have snapshots of all shards available. This behavior can be changed by setting the `partial` parameter to `true`. In this case, only successfully snapshotted shards will be restored and all missing shards will be recreated as empty. Also, you can rename the index that needs to be restored using a regular expression with the `rename_pattern` and `rename_replacement` parameters. In the preceding use, the index named my_index will be restored with `restored_index` name.

When an index restore operation is performed on an existing and open index, it will fail:

```
{
    "error": "SnapshotRestoreException[[my_backup:first_snapshot]
cannot restore index [my_index] because it's open]",
    "status": 500
}
```

You can close the index before the restore operation, as follows:

```
curl -XPOST localhost:9200/my_index/_close
```

Closed indices are opened during the restore operation. Elasticsearch creates new indices if they didn't exist in the cluster. The restore operation uses the Elasticsearch standard shard recovery mechanism. Therefore, if you want to cancel a restore operation that is running, you can use index delete command on the indices that are being restored.

Overriding index settings during restore

Elasticsearch allows you to override most of index settings during the restore process. For example, you can override a number of replica set settings or automatic refresh time settings of the snapshot of an index that will be restored:

```
curl -XPOST localhost:9200/_snapshot/my_backup/first_snapshot/_restore
-d '{
"indices": "my_index",
  "index_settings": {
    "index.number_of_replicas": 2
  },
  "ignore_index_settings": [
      "index.refresh_interval"
  ]
}'
```

By the preceding command, the my_index will be created with two replica shards and a default value of the index refresh interval.

How does the snapshot process works?

As stated earlier, a repository can contain multiple snapshots of the same cluster. Therefore, the snapshots files are stored in compact form. This means that your data will not be repeated when you have multiple snapshots of the same indices. At first, Elasticsearch checks the list of the index files. Then, it copies only newly created or changed files since the last snapshot. Now look at the following example:

```
curl -XGET localhost:9200/my_index/_search?pretty
{
    "took": 3,
    "timed_out": false,
    "_shards": {
        "total": 1,
        "successful": 1,
        "failed": 0
    },
    "hits": {
        "total": 2,
        "max_score": 1,
        "hits": [
            {
                "_index": "my_index",
                "_type": "snapshot",
                "_id": "AVCmN4l-7pWKrBPkopj3",
                "_score": 1,
                "_source": {
                    "title": "Document A"
                }
            },
            {
                "_index": "my_index",
                "_type": "snapshot",
                "_id": "AVCmN5iN7pWKrBPkopj4",
                "_score": 1,
                "_source": {
                    "title": "Document B"
                }
            }
        ]
    }
}
```

We have an index named my_index and it stores two documents. Let's create a snapshot of this index for now as follows:

```
curl -XPUT localhost:9200/_snapshot/my_backup/first_snapshot -d '{
    "indices": "my_index",
    "ignore_unavailable": false,
```

```
    "include_global_state": true,
    "partial": true
}'
{"accepted":true}
```

Now let's add another document to the index:

```
curl -XPOST localhost:9200/my_index/snapshot -d '{
    "title": "Document C"
}'
```

And now let's create a new snapshot again for this index:

```
curl -XPUT localhost:9200/_snapshot/my_backup/second_snapshot -d '{
    "indices": "my_index",
    "ignore_unavailable": false,
    "include_global_state": true,
    "partial": true
}'
{"accepted":true}
```

Let's now get for information about the two snapshots that we created:

```
curl -XGET localhost:9200/_snapshot/my_backup/first_snapshot/_status
{
    "snapshots": [
        {
            "snapshot": "first_snapshot",
            "repository": "kodcucomfs",
            "state": "SUCCESS",
            "shards_stats": {
                "initializing": 0,
                "started": 0,
                "finalizing": 0,
                "done": 1,
                "failed": 0,
                "total": 1
            },
            "stats": {
                "number_of_files": 7,
                "processed_files": 7,
                "total_size_in_bytes": 5059,
                "processed_size_in_bytes": 5059,
                "start_time_in_millis": 1445897714549,
                "time_in_millis": 7
            },
```

. . .

```
curl -XGET localhost:9200/_snapshot/my_backup/second_snapshot/_status
{
    "snapshots": [
        {
            "snapshot": "second_snapshot",
            "repository": "kodcucomfs",
            "state": "SUCCESS",
            "shards_stats": {
                "initializing": 0,
                "started": 0,
                "finalizing": 0,
                "done": 1,
                "failed": 0,
                "total": 1
            },
            "stats": {
                "number_of_files": 4,
                "processed_files": 4,
                "total_size_in_bytes": 2667,
                "processed_size_in_bytes": 2667,
                "start_time_in_millis": 1445897737400,
                "time_in_millis": 7
            },
...
```

As you can see, the size of first_snapshot is approximately twice the size of second_snapshot. The reason is that my_index had two documents during the first_snapshot creation. We have created the second_snapshot after adding the third document in the my_index. So, the second_snapshot includes reference to one document while the first_snapshot includes reference to two documents. This intelligent behavior saves time and system resources.

Summary

In this chapter, we looked at how to back up and restore our data. For this reason, we examined the snapshot repository, and then we looked at how to create a snapshot and restore it. We talked about their configuration details. Finally, we discussed how snapshot process works. In the next chapter, we will examine how to improve the user search experience. We will look at how you can correct spelling mistakes and we will examine the suggest API. Finally, we will discuss the improving query relevance and we will look at some relevant cases related to this topic.

8

Improving the User Search Experience

In the previous chapter, we looked at how to back up and restore our data. We examined the snapshot repository and snapshot/restore process functionality. We talked about configuration details to snapshot and restore. Finally, we discussed how the snapshot process works and the form of snapshot files. In this chapter, we will examine the Elasticsearch Suggest API to correct user's spelling mistakes and we will look closely at the various functionalities provided by Elasticsearch to improve the relevancy of search results. By the end of this chapter, we will have covered:

- How to correct user's spelling mistakes
- How to use the term suggester
- How to use the phrase suggester
- How to provide the autocomplete functionality for the user
- How to use boosting
- How to use synonyms

Correction of users' spelling mistakes

Typos and spelling mistakes are often encountered due to many reasons. Therefore, correcting typos and user spelling mistakes is an integral part of a good search experience. When you search for a phrase that is close to another frequently searched phrase, you may see the **did you mean** phrase, which helps correct users' spelling mistakes, as search engines use this form to improve the user search experience. For such a case, this is what Google shows us when we type in **threat safe** instead of **thread safe**. Take a look at the following screenshot as an example:

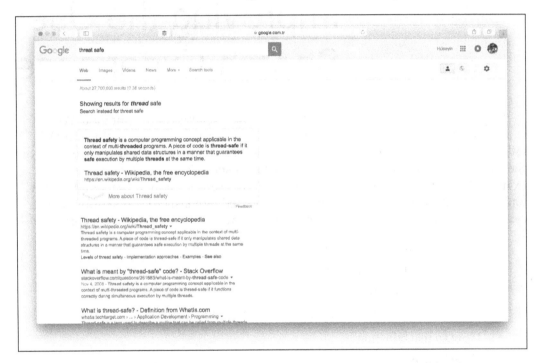

Elasticsearch allows us to use the **Suggest API** functionality. In this section, we will look at how to use the Suggest API both in simple use case scenarios and the basic configuration settings.

Suggesters

The Suggest API suggests similar terms based on text that you provided by using a suggester. Elasticsearch allows us to use three suggesters that provide three different functionalities. These are **term**, **phrase**, and **completion**. The term and phrase suggesters allow us to correct spelling mistakes. The completion suggester provides the autocomplete functionality. A suggestion request can be used in two ways:

- Using the REST _suggest endpoint
- Defined alongside the query part of a _search request

Now, let's examine how we can use these formats.

Using the _suggest REST endpoint

When using the _suggest REST endpoint, you must provide text for suggestions and the type of the suggester to use. Endpoint provides suggestions that are similar to the text provided. The following is an example of the _suggest REST endpoint. We would like to get suggestions for the word jama. Of course, we've misspelled it on purpose to understand the suggestion's working logic:

```
curl -XGET localhost:9200/my_index/_suggest?pretty -d '{
  "my_suggestion" : {
    "text : "jama",
    "term" : {
      "field : "_all"
    }
  }
}'
```

In the preceding example, first we specified a name for the suggestion request. In this example, it is my_suggestion. Then, we specified the text that we want to suggest to be returned by using the text parameter. Afterward, we added the suggester type. Here, a term suggester is used. The term suggester object contains its configuration, and the field property defines the field that we want to use for suggestions. In this example, we specified that we wanted to use the _all field. Now, let's look at the example response:

```
{
  "_"shards":" {
    "total":" 5,
    "successful":" 5,
    "failed":" 0
  },
  "my_suggestion":" [
```

```
{
    "text": """jama","
    "offset":" 0,
    "length":" 4,
    "options":" [
        {
            "text": "java",
            "score":" 0.75,
            "freq":" 415
        },
        {
            "text": "jaka",
            "score":" 0.75,
            "freq":" 109
        },
        {
            "text": "jakas",
            "score":" 0.5,
            "freq":" 37
        },
        {
            "text": "j2me",
            "score":" 0.5,
            "freq":" 26
        },
        {
            "text": "jakao",
            "score":" 0.5,
            "freq":" 13
        }
    ]
}
]
}
```

As you can see in the preceding response, the output returns a list of suggestions for the text provided (that is, term) to us that was present in the text parameter of our my_suggestion section. The term suggester will return an array of possible suggestions with additional information for each term. Looking at the data returned for the term jama, we can see the options array that contains suggestions.

In other words, each entry in this array is a suggestion for the provided term. If Elasticsearch does not find any suggestions for the provided term, the `options` field will be empty. Properties and their meanings are as follows in each matching term object of the options array that is returned by Elasticsearch:

- **Text**: A text parameter of the suggestion for the term provided by user.

- **Score**: The score of the suggestion. The score is a factor indicating how close the suggestion is to the provided term. The higher score can mean a better suggestion. Note that the terms `java` and `jaka` received the highest score according to the preceding response.

- **Frequency**: The frequency of the suggestion. The frequency indicates how many times the term appears in the documents of an index. When you see high frequency, this means that more documents will have the suggested term in their fields and that the suggested term is an appropriate suggestion for users. Note that the term `java` received the highest frequency value according to the preceding response.

In addition, keep in mind that you can send more than one suggestion at a time by adding multiple suggestion names. For example, in addition to the term `jama`, we can also ask for a suggestion for *rumy* (of course, we have again made a misspelling on purpose), as shown here:

```
curl -XGET localhost:9200/my_index/_suggest?pretty -d '{
  "first_suggestion" : {
    "text : "jama",
    "term" : {
      "field : "_all
    }
  },
  "second_suggestion" : {
  "text : "rumy",
  "term" : {
   "field : "_all
  }
  }
}'
```

Suggest object inclusion in the query

A suggest request can be defined alongside the query part of the `_search` request, as follows:

```
curl -XGET localhost:9200/my_index/_search?pretty -d '{
  "query": {
```

```
    "match": {
      "description": """"java"
    }
  },
  "suggest" : {
   "first_suggestion" : {
     "text : "j2se",
     "term" : {
       "field : "_all
     }
   }
  }
 }''
```

Unlike the `_suggest` REST endpoint use, when we include suggestion requests in a query, the documents are also returned to us with the suggestions even if we do not specify the query (the `match_all` query executed by Elasticsearch in this case). At this point, it is important to know that the returned suggestions are independent of the returned result by the specified query.

As we mentioned at the beginning of the *Suggesters* section, Elasticsearch allows us to use three suggesters. Now that we now know how to use a suggestion request with the REST `_suggest` endpoint and as part of a search request, now let's examine these three suggesters.

Term suggester

The term suggester suggests terms based on the edit distance. An edit distance refers to the number of characters that would need to be changed to make the terms match. A term with a lower distance number is considered to be a better match than a term with a higher distance number. Consider the case of `jama` returning to `java` that we previously examined. In order to change the term `jama` to `java`, we need to change the letter `m` to `v`, so this means a distance of 1. The text provided for suggestion is analyzed before terms are suggested, and the terms suggested by Elasticsearch are indicated as per the provided and suggested text.

> The term suggester does not take the query into account even when it is a part of a request.

Configuring the term suggester

Elasticsearch provides many configuration properties to configure the term suggester in order to suit our needs. Now we will talk about these configuration properties.

Common suggest options

The following options can be used for all the suggesters. The available options are:

- `text`: The suggest text. We want to receive suggestions for the text itself. This option is required and can be set globally or as per the suggestion.

- `field`: The field option determines which field to use to fetch the suggestions. It is another required option and it can be set globally or as per the suggestion.

- `analyzer`: This option's value must be an analyzer name that can be used to analyze the text provided in the text parameter. If a value is not set, Elasticsearch will use the search analyzer of the `suggest` field.

- `size`: This option defines the maximum number of suggestions that need to be returned as per the suggest text token. The default value is 5.

- `sort`: This option allows us to specify how suggestions are sorted in the result returned by Elasticsearch. There are two values available — **score** and **frequency**. The default value is `score`. When the `score` value is used, the suggestions will be sorted based on the score first, then the frequency, and then the term itself. If the frequency is used, the suggestions will be sorted by frequency first, then by the similarity score, and then by the term itself.

- `suggest_mode`: This option allows us to control which suggestions will be included in the Elasticsearch response. There are three values available: **missing**, **popular**, and **always**. The default value is `missing`. When `missing` is used, Elasticsearch will generate suggestions for the provided term in the text parameter only if it does not exist in the index. If the value called "popular" is used, Elasticsearch will only suggest terms that exist in more documents than the original term. Or, when the last possible value `always` is used, Elasticsearch will suggest any matching suggestions for each of the words in the text parameter.

Other and additional term suggester options

In addition to the common suggest options, there are additional options we can use for the term suggester. These options are:

- `lowercase_terms`: When this option is set to `true`, Elasticsearch will make all suggest terms lowercase after analysis.

- `max_edits`: This option defines the value of the maximum edit distance and can only take a value between 1 and 2. The default value is 2. When setting this value to 1, you can see fewer but better suggestions in the result.

- `prefix_length`: This option allows us to set how many of the suggestion prefix characters must match the prefix characters of the provided term. The default value is 1. Increasing this number improves spellcheck's performance because usually, spelling mistakes do not appear at the beginning of a word.

- `min_word_length`: This option defines the minimum length of a suggestion that is to be returned. The default value is 4.

- `shard_size`: This option defines the maximum number of suggestions that will be read from each individual shard. The default value is specified by the size parameter. The terms are partitioned among the shards (unless we have a single shard index created) because of the sharding process. Therefore, if you set this option to a value higher than the size parameter, it can be useful in creating a more accurate document frequency.

- `max_inspections`: This option is a factor that defines how many candidates Elasticsearch will look at in order to find the terms on the shard level that can be used as suggestions. The default value is 5. The factor will be used as a multiplier for the `shards_size` option. Setting a higher value than the default value can improve accuracy, but it leads to a cost in performance.

- `min_doc_freq`: This option allows us to define the low limit for the number of documents to appear. For example, if you set the option to 2, this means the suggestion must appear in at least two documents in a given shard. Note that this value is counted per shard, and is not globally counted as one. This option's default value is 0, which means the option is not enabled. When we set option's values higher than 0, it can improve the quality of suggestions returned by only suggesting high frequency terms. This option can be specified as a percentage for lower values than 1. For example, 0.02 means 2%. The shard level document frequencies are used for this option.

- `max_term_freq`: This option defines the maximum number of documents that a suggest text token can exist in order to be included for spellchecking. Similar to the `min_doc_freq` parameter, it can either be a relative percentage number (for example, 0.4 means 4%) or can be provided as an absolute number. This value is per shard frequency. When a value higher than 1 is specified, then a fractional value cannot be specified. The default value is 0.01. If you define a higher value for this option, the overall performance of the spellchecker will be better. In addition, this option is very useful as it excludes high frequency terms from being spellchecked, which are usually correct terms. The shard level document frequencies are used for this option.

The phrase suggester

The phrase suggester is an extended version of the term suggester. It uses *n-gram language models* to calculate how good the suggestion is and selects entire corrected phrases instead of individual weighted tokens. This means that whole phrases will be returned instead of individual terms. The n-gram approach gets a contiguous sequence of N terms from a given text. In other words, it divides terms in the string into grams. For example, if we would like to divide the word Elasticsearch into bi-grams, it would look like this (when a two letter n-gram is used): el la as st ti ic cs se ea ar rc ch.

 If you want more information about the n-gram language models, please see http://en.wikipedia.org/wiki/Language_model#N-gram_models.

The best way to describe the phrase suggester is an example so you can see it in action. We need to create test data for this reason. Let's start by indexing five simple documents:

```
curl -XPOST 'localhost:9200/my_index/article/1' -d '{"title":
"Introduction to ElasticSearch Data Analytics"}'
curl -XPOST 'localhost:9200/my_index/article/2' -d '{"title": "Big
Data search and analysis by ElasticSearch"}'
curl -XPOST 'localhost:9200/my_index/article/3' -d '{"title": "Real-
time Data Analytics with Elasticsearch "}'
curl -XPOST 'localhost:9200/my_index/article/4' -d '{"title": "Data
Mining with ElasticSearch Data Analytics"}'
curl -XPOST 'localhost:9200/my_index/article/5' -d '{"title":
"Elasticsearch Analytics with Kibana"}'
Okay, let's see how we run a phrase suggester request at now:
curl -XPOST localhost:9200/my_index/_search?pretty -d '{
  "size": 0,
  "suggest": {
   "text": "elasticsarch data analytis",
      "phrase_suggestion" : {
        "phrase": {
          "field": "title"
      }
    }
  }
}'
```

When we examine the preceding command, we can see that it is not very different from the command that we ran for the term suggester, except that we specified the phrase type instead of the term type. The response to the preceding command is as follows:

```
{
    "took": 15,
    "timed_out": false,
    "_shards": {
        "total": 5,
        "successful": 5,
        "failed": 0
    },
    "hits": {
        "total": 5,
        "max_score": 0,
        "hits": []
    },
    "suggest": {
        "phrase_suggestion": [
            {
                "text": "elasticsarch data analytis",
                "offset": 0,
                "length": 26,
                "options": [
                    {
                        "text": "elasticsearch data analytics",
                        "score": 0.114973485
                    },
                    {
                        "text": "elasticsearch data analytis",
                        "score": 0.08818061
                    },
                    {
                        "text": "elasticsarch data analytics",
                        "score": 0.08641694
                    },
                    {
                        "text": "elasticsearch data analysis",
                        "score": 0.070414856
                    }
                ]
            }
        ]
    }
}
```

As you can see, when the phrase suggester is used, Elasticsearch will be the whole phrase returned from the document instead of a single word/term for each term from the `text` field. The returning array includes the most likely corrected spelling suggestions and is sorted based on their score. In this case, we first received the expected correction from the Elasticsearch data analytics, while the second correction is relatively less successful in that only one of the errors is corrected.

Note that the request is executed with the `max_errors` parameter even if we did not specify this explicitly. This parameter defines the corrections to be returned with how many misspelled terms there are. There are misspelled terms in the returned array. The default value of this parameter is `1.0`. Now, let's look at what parameters of the phrase suggester are available for usage.

Configuring the phrase suggester

As mentioned earlier, the phrase suggester has been extended from the term suggester. This means there is an inheritance relationship between the phrase suggester and the term suggester, plus the phrase suggester has all the features of the term suggester. Therefore, the phrase suggester can also make use of the common configuration options provided by the term suggester (refer to the *Common suggest options* section in this chapter). In addition to these features, the phrase suggester exposes the following basic options:

- `field`: This option determines which field to use to fetch the suggestions that we use to perform n-gram lookups for the language model. It is a required option.

- `gram_size`: This option defines the maximum size of the n-grams in the field that is specified by the field option. If the specified field does not contain n-grams, this option should be set to 1 or be omitted. This behavior is recommended because Elasticsearch will try to detect the gram size by itself when this option is not set.

- `real_word_error_likelihood`: This option defines the possibility of a term being a misspelled even if the term exists in the index. The default value is 0.95, corresponding to 5%, which tells Elasticsearch that 5% of all the terms that exist in its index are misspelled. Note that when given a low value, this option will result in more terms being taken as misspelled even though they may be correct.

- `confidence`: This option defines a threshold value for suggestion candidates that will be included in the result. For example, when the confidence value is 1.0, Elasticsearch will only return suggestions that score higher than this. If it is set to 0.0, Elasticsearch will result in returning all the suggestions no matter what their scores are with the limited size parameter. The default value is 1.0.

- `max_errors`: This option defines the maximum percentage of terms that can be misspellings in order to create a correction. This option accepts an integer number or a float value in the range between 0 and 1, which will be treated as a percentage value. The default value is 1.0, which means that at most, one misspelled term is returned for only one correction. When a float value is used, it will specify the percentage of terms that can be erroneous. If we specify an integer number, Elasticsearch will treat it as a maximum number of misspelled terms. When given too high a value, this option can negatively affect performance.

- `separator`: This option defines the separator that will be used to divide terms in the bigram field. The whitespace character is used as a separator when this option is not set.

- `highlight`: This option allow us to use suggestions highlighting. When it is being configured, `pre_tag` and `post_` tag should be used to specify which prefix and postfix should be used. For example, if we would like to surround the suggestions with the `<em>` and `</em>` tags, we should set the `pre_` tag to `<em>` and the `post_` tag to `</em>`.

- `collate`: This option allows us to check each suggestion against a specified query or filter to prune suggestions for which no matching documents exist in the index. The query or filter must be specified with this option and it is run as a template query. The query or filter must contain the `{{suggestion}}` variable. The current suggestion is automatically made usable on this variable. Also, you can specify your own template `params`. When the additional parameter called `prune` is set to `true`, the suggestions will have an additional option called `collate_match`. The default value of `prune` is `false`.

Now let's look at an example of using some of the parameters mentioned earlier. For example, if you want to use highlighting the command, it would look as follows:

```
curl -XPOST localhost:9200/my_index/_search -d '{
  "size": 0,
  "suggest": {
  "text": "elasticsarch data analytis",
      "phrase_suggestion" : {
        "phrase": {
          "field": "title",
          "real_word_error_likelihood" : 0.95,
          "max_errors" : 0.5,
          "highlight": {
          "pre_tag": "<em>",
          "post_tag": "</em>"
        },
```

```
              "collate" : {
                  "prune" : true,
                  "query" : {
                    "match" : {
                      "{{field}}": "{{suggestion}}"
                    }
                  },
                  "params": {
                    "field": "title"
                  }
              }
          }
        }
      }
    }
}'
```

The result returned by Elasticsearch for the preceding query would be as follows:

```
{
    "took": 17,
    "timed_out": false,
    "_shards": {
        "total": 5,
        "successful": 5,
        "failed": 0
    },
    "hits": {
        "total": 5,
        "max_score": 0,
        "hits": []
    },
    "suggest": {
        "phrase_suggestion": [
            {
                "text": "elasticsarch data analytis",
                "offset": 0,
                "length": 26,
                "options": [
                    {
                        "text": "elasticsearch data analytics",
                        "highlighted": "<em>elasticsearch</em> data
<em>analytics</em>",
                        "score": 0.114973485,
                        "collate_match": true
                    },
```

```
                {
                        "text": "elasticsearch data analytis",
                        "highlighted": "<em>elasticsearch</em> data
        analytis",
                        "score": 0.08818061,
                        "collate_match": true
                },
                {
                        "text": "elasticsarch data analytics",
                        "highlighted": "elasticsarch data <em>analytics</
        em>",
                        "score": 0.08641694,
                        "collate_match": true
                },
                {
                        "text": "elasticsearch data analysis",
                        "highlighted": "<em>elasticsearch</em> data
        <em>analysis</em>",
                        "score": 0.070414856,
                        "collate_match": true
                }
            ]
        }
      ]
    }
}
```

As expected, the suggestions were highlighted nicely.

The completion suggester

The completion suggester provides a basic auto complete functionality instead of doing spell correction, unlike other suggesters. Actually, it is a so-called prefix suggester based on the **Finite State Transducer (FST)** data structure. In this structure, available suggestions can be stored as more than one output value for each input string value.

 If you want more information on the FTS data structure, please refer to http://en.wikipedia.org/wiki/ Finite_state_transducer.

Prefix suggestions are faster than other suggestions. They are stored on an FTS-like data structure as part of your index during index time. For this reason, the completion suggester allows really fast loads and executions of the suggestions because it does not perform any calculations during query time.

Mapping the configuration for the completion suggester

In order to use this feature, we need to dedicate one field, which will be called **completion** and we have to specify a special mapping for it. Thus, the field stores the FST-like structure in the index. In order to illustrate how to use this suggester, let's create an index to search for movie directors with the autocomplete feature. Next to a director's name, we want to return the identifiers of the movie she/he directed in order to search for them with an additional query. We create the director's index by running the following command:

```
curl -XPOST localhost:9200/imdb -d '{
  "mappings": {
    "director": {
      "properties": {
       "name": {
           "type": "string"
       },
       "completion_suggest": {
        "type": "completion",
        "analyzer": "simple",
        "search_analyzer": "simple",
        "payloads": true
       }
      }
     }
    }
  }'
{"acknowledged":"true}
```

Okay. Now we have an index, and it will contain a single type called "director." We specified two fields for each document, which will be stored under this type. These fields are the name and completion_suggest. The first field is the name of the director and the second field is the field we will use for the autocomplete function. Note that we defined the completion_suggest field using the completion type, which will result in storing the FST-like structure in the index. The mapping of the completion suggester supports the following parameters:

- type: This option is required and should be set to completion.

- `analyzer`: This option defines the analyzer to use during indexing time. The default value is `simple`.

- `search_analyzer`: This option defines the analyzer to use during query time. The value is value of analyzer.

- `payloads`: This option defines whether or not stores for payloads. The default value is `false`. It allows you to return additional information along with the suggestion when set to `true`.

- `preserve_separators`: This option defines whether or not the separators are taken into consideration. The default value is `true`. For example, when it is set to `false`, you could find a field starting with Real Madrid if you suggest for `realm`.

- `preserve_position_increments`: This option defines whether or not the position increments are enabled. The default value is `true`. For example, when it is set to `false`, you could find a field starting with The Godfather, if you suggest `g`.

- `max_input_length`: This option defines the limit for the length of a single input. The default value is 50 UTF-16 code points.

Indexing on completion field

We will now index a document describing Andrei Tarkovsky, and we will provide some additional information about his movies. Let's look at the following code:

```
curl -XPOST localhost:9200/imdb/director/1 -d '{
  "name": "Andrei Tarkovsky",
  "completion_suggest": {
   "input": [ "andrei", "arsenyevich", "tarkovsky" ],
   "output": "Andrei Arsenyevich Tarkovsky",
   "payload": { "movies" : [ "Ivan's Childhood", "Andrei Rublev",
"Solaris", "The Mirror", "Stalker", "Nostalgia", "The Sacrifice" ] }
  }
}'
{"_"index":"""imdb","_"""type":"""director","_"""id":"""1","_""version":
"1,"created":"true}
```

As you can see, we provided the input, output, and payload properties for the `completion_suggest` field. The following parameters are supported:

- `input`: This field stores the input. It can be an array of strings or just a string. This field is required.

- `output`: This field stores a string to return when a suggestion matches. This field is optional.

- payload: This field stores a JSON object to return additional information about your document as arbitrary and is optional.

- weight: This field stores a positive integer or a string containing a positive integer value to define a weight related to the document. It allows you to rank your suggestions and is optional.

Get suggestions

If we would like to find documents that have directors starting with tar, we would run the following command:

```
curl -XGET localhost:9200/imdb/_suggest?pretty -d '{
  "directorAutocomplete": {
   "text": "tar",
   "completion": {
    "field": "completion_suggest"
   }
  }
}'
```

The result returned by Elasticsearch for the preceding query looks as follows:

```
{
    "_shards": {
       "total": 5,
       "successful": 5,
       "failed": 0
    },
    "directorAutocomplete": [
       {
          "text": "tar",
          "offset": 0,
          "length": 3,
          "options": [
             {
                "text": "Andrei Arsenyevich Tarkovsky",
                "score": 1,
                "payload": {
                   "movies": [
                      "Ivan's Childhood",
                      "Andrei Rublev",
                      "Solaris",
                      "The Mirror",
```

```
                    "Stalker",
                    "Nostalgia",
                    "The Sacrifice"
              ]
            }
          }
        ]
      }
    ]
  }
```

As you can see, the document about Andrei Tarkovsky has been returned to us with the payload information about his movies when we search for the phrase `tar` because we indexed the phrases `andrei`, `arsenyevich`, and `tarkovsky` in the document's completion field as input values. This is why the phrase `tar` matched the phrase `tarkovsky` and the text (that is, `Andrei Tarkovsky Arsenyevich`) that is indexed as the output value is returned to us with the `payload` field.

Improving the relevancy of search results

In general, Elasticsearch is used for searching while it is a data analysis tool. In this respect, improving query relevance is an important issue. Of course, searching also means querying and scoring, thus it is a very important part of querying in Apache Lucene as well. We can use the re-scoring mechanism to improve the query's relevance. In addition to the capabilities of document scoring in the Apache Lucene library, Elasticsearch provides different query types to manipulate the score of the results returned by our queries. In this section, you will find several tips on this issue.

Boosting the query

Boosting queries allows us to effectively demote results that match a given query. This feature is very useful in that we can send some irrelevant records of the result set to the back. For example, we have an index that stores the skills of developers and we're looking for developers who know the Java language. We use a query such as the following for this case:

```
curl -XGET localhost:9200/my_index/_search?pretty -d '{
  "fields": ["age", "skills", "education_status"],
  "query": {
    "match": {
      "skills": "java"
    }
  }
}
```

```
}'
...
        {
            "_index": "my_index",
            "_type": "talent",
            "_id": "AVERYloLvXHAFW5Vn9ct",
            "_score": 0.30685282,
            "fields": {
                "skills": [
                    "c++",
                    "ruby",
                    "java",
                    "scala",
                    "python"
                ],
                "education_status": [
                    "graduated"
                ],
                "age": [
                    26
                ]
            }
        },
        {
            "_index": "my_index",
            "_type": "talent",
            "_id": "AVERZkNpvXHAFW5Vn9jo",
            "_score": 0.30685282,
            "fields": {
                "skills": [
                    "java",
                    "jsf",
                    "wicket",
                    "scala",
                    "python",
                    "play",
                    "spring"
                ],
                "education_status": [
                    "student"
                ],
                "age": [
                    22
                ]
```

```
                    }
                },
                {
                    "_index": "my_index",
                    "_type": "talent",
                    "_id": "AVERXyjCvXHAFW5Vn9W9",
                    "_score": 0.30685282,
                    "fields": {
                        "skills": [
                            "c",
                            "java",
                            "spring",
                            "spring mvc",
                            "node.js"
                        ],
                        "education_status": [
                            "graduated"
                        ],
                        "age": [
                            27
                        ]
                    }
                }
            }
```

What can we do if there are some documents returned that we don't care as much about than other documents, and what can we do in order to discover the most relevant records first while browsing through the data? For example, we want to prioritize students. Reducing the score of documents that have unwanted terms could be a solution. You can specify negative rules in a `bool` query. In this case, the documents containing unwanted terms are still returned, but their overall scores are reduced. To send such a query to Elasticsearch, we will use the following command:

```
curl -XGET localhost:9200/my_index/_search?pretty -d '{
    "fields": ["age", "skills", "education_status"],
    "query": {
        "boosting": {
            "positive": {
                "match": {
                    "skills": "java"
                }
            },
            "negative": {
                "match": {
                    "education_status": "graduated"
                }
```

```
        },
    "negative_boost": 0.2
      }
    }
  }'
  ...
          {
              "_index": "my_index",
              "_type": "talent",
              "_id": "AVERZkNpvXHAFW5Vn9jo",
              "_score": 0.30685282,
              "_source": {
                  "age": 22,
                  "skills": [
                      "java",
                      "jsf",
                      "wicket",
                      "scala",
                      "python",
                      "play",
                      "spring"
                  ],
                  "education_status": "student"
              }
          },
          {
              "_index": "my_index",
              "_type": "talent",
              "_id": "AVERYloLvXHAFW5Vn9ct",
              "_score": 0.061370563,
              "_source": {
                  "age": 26,
                  "skills": [
                      "c++",
                      "ruby",
                      "java",
                      "scala",
                      "python"
                  ],
                  "education_status": "graduated"
              }
          },
          {
```

```
   "_index": "my_index",
           "_type": "talent",
           "_id": "AVERXyjCvXHAFW5Vn9W9",
           "_score": 0.061370563,
           "_source": {
               "age": 27,
               "skills": [
                   "c",
                   "java",
                   "spring",
                   "spring mvc",
                   "node.js"
               ],
               "education_status": "graduated"
           }
       }
   }
```

As you can see, the score of the document whose `education_status` field value
is `student` is the same as the previous query result, but the scores of the last two
documents have been decreased by 80 %. The reason is that it has been changed in
terms of the value of the negative boost. We set its value to `0.2` in the preceding
command.

Bool query

The `bool` query allows us to use Boolean combinations in nested queries. It provides
a should occurrence type that defines no must clauses in a Boolean query (of course,
this behavior can be changed by setting the `minimum_should_match` parameter),
but each matching `should` clause increases the document score. This feature is very
useful when you want to move some results among the result set to the forefront. For
example, we have an index that stores technical articles and we're looking for articles
written about `Docker`. We use a query like the following for this:

```
curl -XGET localhost:9200/my_index/_search -d '{
  "query": {
    "multi_match": {
      "query": "docker",
      "fields": ["_all"]
    }
  }
}'
...
          {
              "_index": "my_index",
```

```
                "_type": "article",
                "_id": "AVETmMSTOCXTx0WbQQh1",
                "_score": 0.13005449,
                "_source": {
                    "title": "9 Open Source DevOps Tools We Love",
                    "content": "We have configured Jenkins to build code,
    create Docker containers..."
                }
            },
            {
                "_index": "my_index",
                "_type": "article",
                "_id": "AVET1_kKOCXTx0WbQQga",
                "_score": 0.111475274,
                "_source": {
                    "title": "Using Docker Volume Plugins with Amazon ECS-
    Optimized AMI",
                    "content": "Amazon EC2 Container Service (ECS) is a
    highly scalable, high performance container management services..."
                }
            }
        ...
```

As you can see, the first document seems less relevant for docker compared to the second document. In this case, we can use a should clause, plus we can use the boost parameter to improve the relevancy of our search results. The boost parameter allows us to increase the weight of the given fields. Thus, it tells Elasticsearch that some fields are more important than other fields when performing term matching. If the title field contains the term that we're looking for, the document is relevant. This assessment is not wrong. Therefore, in our example, the important field is title. We could run the following command as an another example:

```
curl -XGET localhost:9200/my_index/_search?pretty -d '{
    "query": {
        "bool": {
            "must": [
                {
                    "match": {
                        "_all": "docker"
                    }
                }
            ],
            "should": [
                {
                    "match": {
```

```
                "title": {
                   "query": "docker",
                   "boost": 2
                }
            }
         }
       }
     ]
   }
 }
}'
```

Okay, let's now look at the example response:

```
    . . .

       {
          "_index": "my_index",
          "_type": "article",
          "_id": "AVET1_kKOCXTx0WbQQga",
          "_score": 0.33130926,
          "_source": {
             "title": "Using Docker Volume Plugins with Amazon ECS-
   Optimized AMI",
             "content": "Amazon EC2 Container Service (ECS) is a
   highly scalable, high performance container management services..."
          }
       },
       {
          "_index": "my_index",
          "_type": "article",
          "_id": "AVETmMSTOCXTx0WbQQh1",
          "_score": 0.018529123,
          "_source": {
             "title": "9 Open Source DevOps Tools We Love",
             "content": "We have configured Jenkins to build code,
   create Docker containers..."
          }
       }
    . . .
```

As you can see, the first document returned is now more relevant with regard to the should clause and the boost parameter.

Synonyms

We talked about subtle analysis in the *Introduction to Analysis* section in *Chapter 4, Analysis and Analyzers*. Recall what you learned about the topic: TR relates to Turkey and a search for Jeffrey Jacob Abrams also relates to J.J. Abrams. The simpler and more subtle the changes, the easier it is for human beings to notice this similarity. However, the machines need assistance here. Synonyms allow us to ensure that documents are found with terms of the same/similar meanings in this regard. In other words, they are used to broaden the scope of what is considered as a matching document. Now let's examine the following example:

```
curl -XPUT localhost:9200/travel -d '{
  "settings": {
    "analysis": {
      "filter": {
        "tr_synonym_filter": {
          "type": "synonym",
          "synonyms": [
            "tr,turkey"
          ]
        }
      },
      "analyzer": {
        "tr_synonyms": {
          "tokenizer": "standard",
          "filter": [
            "lowercase",
            "tr_synonym_filter"
          ]
        }
      }
    }
  },
  "mappings": {
    "city": {
      "properties": {
        "city": {
          "type": "string", "analyzer": "tr_synonyms"
        },
        "description": {
          "type": "string", "analyzer": "tr_synonyms"
        }
      }
    }
  }
}'
```

We created a travel index using the `tr_synonyms` analyzer. It is configured with the synonym token filter whose name is `tr_synonym_filter`. The `tr_synonym_filter` handles synonyms during the analysis process. Its `synonyms` parameter accepts an array of synonyms that were provided by us. The only element of the array says that `tr` is a synonym of `turkey` and vice versa. Now let's add a document to the index:

```
curl -XPOST localhost:9200/travel/city -d '{
  "city": "Istanbul",
  "description": "Istanbul is the most populous city in Turkey."
}'
{"_"index":"""travel","_""type":"""city","_""id":"""AVEXOA_xXNtV9WrYCp
uZ","_""version":"1,"created":"true}
```

Now, let us search tr phrase on travel index:

```
curl -XGET localhost:9200/travel/_search?pretty -d '{
  "query": {
    "match": {
      "description": "tr"
    }
  }
}'
{
  "took": 12,
  "timed_out": false,
  "_shards": {
    "total": 5,
    "successful": 5,
    "failed": 0
  },
  "hits": {
    "total": 1,
    "max_score": 0.13561106,
    "hits": [
      {
        "_index": "travel",
        "_type": "city",
        "_id": "AVEXOA_xXNtV9WrYCpuZ",
        "_score": 0.13561106,
        "_source": {
          "city": "Istanbul",
          "description": "Istanbul is the most populous city in
Turkey."
        }
      }
    ]
  }
}
```

As you can see, the document that we're looking for was returned to us because the `tr_synonym_filter` handles synonyms by means of the synonyms provided that were defined by us.

Be careful about the _all field

We talked about the _all field in the *_all* section in *Chapter 3, Basic Concepts of Mapping*. To remind you briefly, Elasticsearch allows you to search in all the fields of a document. This facility is provided by the _all field, because it includes the text of one or more other fields within the document indexed and concatenates them into one big string. This feature is very useful when want to use a full-text search. However, due to the structure of the field, we may not produce the expected results when searching on this field. For example, let's change the query to run on the _all field that we used in our previous example:

```
curl -XGET localhost:9200/travel/_search?pretty -d '{
  "query": {
    "match": {
      "_all": "tr"
    }
  }
}'
{
    "took": 15,
    "timed_out": false,
    "_shards": {
       "total": 5,
       "successful": 5,
       "failed": 0
    },
    "hits": {
       "total": 0,
       "max_score": null,
       "hits": []
    }
}
```

As you can see, no document was returned to us in the query results. This is because the _all field combines the original values from each field of the document as a string. In our previous example, the _all field only included these terms: [istanbul, is, the, most, populous, city, in, turkey].

So, similar words did not appear in this field. Another important point to note is that the _all field is of the type string. This means that the fields' values of different types are stored as a string type. For example, if we have a date field whose value is 2002-11-03 00:00:00 UTC, the _all field will contain the terms [2003, 11, and 03].

Summary

In this chapter, we looked at the Suggest API and saw how we can use term, phrase, and completion suggesters with their configuration details. Then, we looked at the various functionalities to improve the relevancy of search results provided by Elasticsearch. We looked at how we can broaden the scope of matching documents with the synonym facility. Finally, we tried to correctly understand the notion of the _all field in depth.

Thank you for reading this book. We hope that you liked it and that we have reinforced your knowledge of effective indexing, which can adeptly help you to improve the relevancy of search results using Elasticsearch.

Index

Symbols

_all field 28, 29
_source field 3-28
_suggest REST endpoint
  suggest object inclusion 127, 128
  used, for correcting users' spelling
    mistakes 125-127
_timestamp field 30-32
_ttl field 32, 33

A

analysis
  about 10, 47-49
  examining 10-15
  normalizing 49
  process 49, 50
  tokenizing 49
analyzer
  custom analyzer, creating 64, 65
  pipeline 60
  specifying, for field in mapping 60-64
Apache Lucene
  about 3, 18
  URL 3
ASCII Folding token filter 54, 56-59
attachment type
  about 38
  reference link 38
AWS Cloud Plugin
  about 114
  URL 114
Azure Cloud Plugin
  about 114
  URL 114

B

big data 1
bool query
  using 144-146
built-in analyzers
  about 50, 51
  building blocks 51
  character filters 51
  Language Analyzer 51
  Pattern Analyzer 51
  Simple Analyzer 50
  Standard Analyzer 50
  Stop Analyzer 51
  token filters 54
  tokenizer 53, 54
  Whitespace Analyzer 50
bulk API 107, 108
bulk sizing 108

C

character filters
  about 51
  HTML Strip Char filter 51-53
  Pattern Replace Char filter 53
client nodes 68
cloud repository 114
completion suggester
  completion field, indexing 138
  configuration, mapping 137, 138
  used, for correcting users' spelling
    mistakes 136
**Concurrent Mark Sweep garbage
    collector** 90

configuration, for high performance indexing
  file descriptors 91
  garbage collector 84
  JVM memory 84
  memory configuration 80
  performing 80
  swapping, avoiding 82
custom analyzer
  creating 64, 65

D

database 2
dedicated master nodes 68
denormalization 21, 22
document
  about 20, 21
  inverted index 23-25
document-oriented search engine 2
document storage
  _source field 3-6
  about 2, 3
  storable field, versus searchable field 6-10

E

Elasticsearch 1
Elasticsearch cluster
  about 67, 68
  architecture, of distribution 70-72
  configuring 73-76
ES_HEAP_SIZE environment variable 81

F

file descriptors
  about 91
  FD limit, increasing on Unix systems 91-93
Finite State Transducer (FST) data structure
  about 136
  URL 136
full text search engine 1

G

garbage collection
  monitoring 86

  tuning 91
garbage collector
  about 84
  Concurrent Mark Sweep garbage collector 90
  G1 garbage collector 90
  parallel garbage collector 90
  serial garbage collector 90
  strategies 89

H

HDFS filesystem repository
  about 114
  URL 114
HTML Strip Char filter 51-53
hybrid filesystem store 106

I

ICU analysis plugin
  about 56
  ASCII Folding token filter 56-59
  reference link 56
indices
  about 17, 18
  mapping 19
  types 19, 20
inverted index 3, 18, 23-25
I/O operations
  throttling 106
  throttling type, configuring 106, 107

J

Java FileChannel Class
  URL 105
Java garbage collection 84
Java RandomAccessFile Class
  URL 104
JavaScript Object Notation (JSON)
  about 17
  reference link 17
JConsole
  URL 86
jstat command
  URL 86

JVM memory
Code Cache 85
deallocating 89
Eden Space 85
garbage collection, monitoring 86
garbage collector 89
garbage collectors, strategies 89
Old Generation 84
Permanent Generation 85
problem 86
structure 84, 85
Survivor Space 85
Tenured Generation 85
VisualVM 87, 88
Young Generation 84

L

Language Analyzer 51
Length Token Filter 54
Letter Tokenizer 54
log_byte_size policy
about 102
settings 102
log_doc policy
about 103
settings 103
Lowercase Token Filter 54
Lucene MMapDirectory
URL 105
Lucene NIOFSDirectory
URL 105
Lucene SimpleFSDirectory
URL 104

M

major GC 85
mapping
about 19, 27
analyzer, specifying for field 60-64
and search results, relationship
between 38-43
metadata fields 28
mapping definition
automatic index refresh time, setting 97
index_option of string type 95

norms 94
optimization 94
unnecessary fields, excluding 96
memory configuration
about 80
ES_HEAP_SIZE environment variable 81
merging policies
about 98-100
log_byte_size policy 102
log_doc policy 103
selecting 100
tiered policy 100, 101
metadata fields
_all 28, 29
_source 28
_timestamp 30-32
_ttl 32, 33
about 28
minor GC 85
mlockall property 83
MMap filesystem store 105

N

new IO filesystem store 105
NFC 55
NFD 55
NFKC 55
NFKD 55
n-gram language models
URL 131
node
about 68
non-data nodes 68
tribe node 69
non-data nodes
client nodes 68
dedicated master nodes 68
Normalization Token Filters 54
normalizing 49

O

object type
about 33-37
root object type 37
optimize API 103

P

parallel garbage collector **90**
Path Hierarchy Tokenizer **54**
Pattern Analyzer **51**
Pattern Replace Char filter **53**
Pattern Tokenizer **54**
phrase suggester
  configuring 133-136
  used, for correcting users' spelling
      mistakes 131-133

R

relevancy, of search results
  _all field, using 149
  bool query, using 144-146
  improving 140
  query, boosting 140-144
  synonyms, using 147-149
replicas
  about 69
  selecting 76, 77
restore
  about 118
  index settings, overriding 119
Reverse Token Filter **54**
root object type **37**

S

schema-less **43-45**
search results
  and mapping, relationship between 38-43
  relevancy, improving 140
segments
  about 98-100
  optimize API 103
serial garbage collector **90**
sharding **18, 69**
shards
  about 18, 69
  selecting 76, 77
shared filesystem repository **112, 113**
Simple Analyzer **50**
simple filesystem store **104**

snapshot
  about 114-118
  process 120-122
snapshot repository
  about 111, 112
  cloud repository 114
  HDFS filesystem repository 114
  shared filesystem repository 112, 113
  types 112
  URL repository 113
Standard Analyzer **50**
Standard Tokenizer **54**
Stop Analyzer **51**
Stop Token Filter **54**
storable field
  versus searchable field 6-10
store module **104**
store types
  about 104
  hybrid filesystem store 106
  MMap filesystem store 105
  new IO filesystem store 105
  simple filesystem store 104
Suggest API **124**
suggesters
  used, for correcting users' spelling
      mistakes 125
suggestions
  obtaining 139, 140
swapping
  avoiding 82
  mlockall property 83
synonyms
  using 147-149

T

term suggester
  additional options 129, 130
  configuration options 129
  configuring 129
  used, for correcting users' spelling
      mistakes 128
text normalization **55**
tiered policy
  about 100, 101
  settings 100, 101

token filters
  about 54
  ASCII Folding Token Filter 54
  Length Token Filter 54
  Lowercase Token Filter 54
  Normalization Token Filters 54
  Reverse Token Filter 54
  Stop Token Filter 54
  Trim Token Filter 54
  Uppercase Token Filter 54
tokenizer
  about 53
  Letter Tokenizer 54
  Path Hierarchy Tokenizer 54
  Pattern Tokenizer 54
  Standard Tokenizer 54
  UAX Email URL Tokenizer 54
  Whitespace Tokenizer 54
tokenizing 49
tribe node 69
types
  about 33
  attachment type 38
  object type 33-37
types, indices 19, 20

U

UAX Email URL Tokenizer 54
Unicode Consortium
  about 12
  URL 12
unicode normalization forms
  URL 55
Unicode Standard Annex #29
  URL 54

Unix systems
  FD limit, increasing on 91-93
Uppercase Token Filter 54
URL repository 113
users' spelling mistakes, correcting
  _suggest REST
    endpoint used 125-127
  about 124
  completion suggester used 136
  phrase suggester used 131-133
  suggesters used 125
  term suggester used 128

V

VirtualLock
  URL 83
Visual GC plugin
  URL 88
VisualVM
  about 87, 88
  URL 88
VM parameter
  -Xmn 80
  -Xms 80
  -Xmx 80
  -XX:InitialSurvivorRatio 80
  -XX:MaxPermSize 80
  -XX:PermSize 80

W

Whitespace Analyzer 50
Whitespace Tokenizer 54

Thank you for buying
Elasticsearch Indexing

About Packt Publishing

Packt, pronounced 'packed', published its first book, *Mastering phpMyAdmin for Effective MySQL Management*, in April 2004, and subsequently continued to specialize in publishing highly focused books on specific technologies and solutions.

Our books and publications share the experiences of your fellow IT professionals in adapting and customizing today's systems, applications, and frameworks. Our solution-based books give you the knowledge and power to customize the software and technologies you're using to get the job done. Packt books are more specific and less general than the IT books you have seen in the past. Our unique business model allows us to bring you more focused information, giving you more of what you need to know, and less of what you don't.

Packt is a modern yet unique publishing company that focuses on producing quality, cutting-edge books for communities of developers, administrators, and newbies alike. For more information, please visit our website at www.packtpub.com.

About Packt Open Source

In 2010, Packt launched two new brands, Packt Open Source and Packt Enterprise, in order to continue its focus on specialization. This book is part of the Packt Open Source brand, home to books published on software built around open source licenses, and offering information to anybody from advanced developers to budding web designers. The Open Source brand also runs Packt's Open Source Royalty Scheme, by which Packt gives a royalty to each open source project about whose software a book is sold.

Writing for Packt

We welcome all inquiries from people who are interested in authoring. Book proposals should be sent to author@packtpub.com. If your book idea is still at an early stage and you would like to discuss it first before writing a formal book proposal, then please contact us; one of our commissioning editors will get in touch with you.

We're not just looking for published authors; if you have strong technical skills but no writing experience, our experienced editors can help you develop a writing career, or simply get some additional reward for your expertise.

ElasticSearch Cookbook
Second Edition

ISBN: 978-1-78355-483-6   Paperback: 472 pages

Over 130 advanced recipes to search, analyze, deploy, manage, and monitor data effectively with ElasticSearch

1. Deploy and manage simple ElasticSearch nodes as well as complex cluster topologies.

2. Write native plugins to extend the functionalities of ElasticSearch to boost your business.

3. Packed with clear, step-by-step recipes to walk you through the capabilities of ElasticSearch.

Elasticsearch for Hadoop

ISBN: 978-1-78528-899-9   Paperback: 222 pages

Integrate Elasticsearch into Hadoop to effectively visualize and analyze your data

1. Build production-ready analytics applications by integrating the Hadoop ecosystem with Elasticsearch.

2. Learn complex Elasticsearch queries and develop real-time monitoring Kibana dashboards to visualize your data.

3. Use Elasticsearch and Kibana to search data in Hadoop easily with this comprehensive, step-by-step guide.

Please check **www.PacktPub.com** for information on our titles

Elasticsearch Blueprints

ISBN: 978-1-78398-492-3   Paperback: 192 pages

A practical project-based guide to generating compelling search solutions using the dynamic and powerful features of Elasticsearch

1. Discover the power of Elasticsearch by implementing it in a variety of real-world scenarios such as restaurant and e-commerce search.

2. Discover how the features you see in an average Google search can be achieved using Elasticsearch.

3. Learn how to not only generate accurate search results, but also improve the quality of searches for relevant results.

Elasticsearch Server
Second Edition

ISBN: 978-1-78398-052-9   Paperback: 428 pages

A practical guide to building fast, scalable, and flexible search solutions with clear and easy-to-understand examples

1. Learn about the fascinating functionality of Elasticsearch such as data indexing, data analysis, and dynamic mapping.

2. Fine-tune Elasticsearch and understand its metrics using its API and available tools, and see how it behaves in complex searches.

3. A hands-on tutorial that walks you through all the features of Elasticsearch in an easy-to-understand way, with examples that will help you become an expert in no time.

Please check **www.PacktPub.com** for information on our titles